/ renew by date shown.

it at:

Paper Sculpt

SENSATION

Marion Elliot

D&C

David and Charles

www.mycraftivity.com

A DAVID & CHARLES BOOK
Copyright © David & Charles Limited 2009

David & Charles is an F+W Media Inc. company
4700 East Galbraith Road
Cincinnati, OH 45236

First published in the UK in 2009

Text and designs copyright © Marion Elliot 2009
Photography and layout © David & Charles 2009

A catalogue record for this book is available
from the British Library.

745.54

ISBN-13: 978-0-7153-2972-6 hardback
ISBN-10: 0-7153-2772-3 hardback
ISBN-13: 978-0-7153-2973-3 paperback
ISBN-10: 0-7153-2973-1 paperback

Printed in China by Shenzhen Donnelley Printing Co. Ltd.
for David & Charles
Brunel House   Newton Abbot   Devon

Senior Commissioning Editor: Cheryl Brown
Editor: Bethany Dymond
Designer: Mia Farrant
Art Director: Sarah Underhill
Project Editor: Jo Richardson
Production Controller: Kelly Smith
Photographers: Kim Sayer and Karl Adamson

Visit our website at
www.davidandcharles.co.uk

David & Charles books are available from all
good bookshops; alternatively you can contact
our Orderline on 0870 9908222 or write to
us at FREEPOST EX2 110, D&C Direct, Newton
Abbot, TQ12 4ZZ (no stamp required UK only);
US customers call 800-289-0963 and Canadian
customers call 800-840-5220.

For all my friends
in Raving Lane

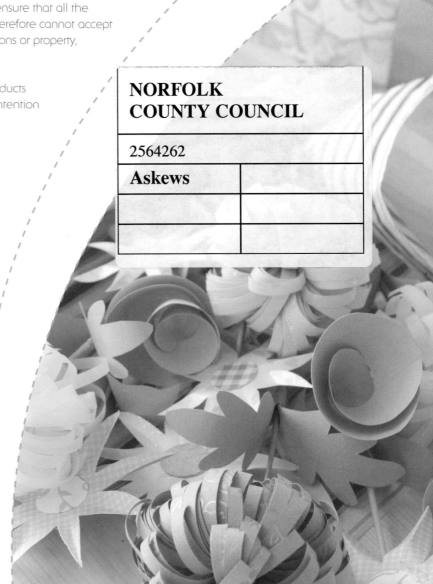

Contents

Introduction

Of all the papercrafting skills, paper sculpture is the one I most enjoy. Taking the humblest of materials and tools – a flat sheet of paper, scissors and glue – then working out how to make something three-dimensional with them is a challenge that I really love. I do hope that the projects presented in this book will inspire the same excitement in you, and convince you that you too can have just as much fun as I do with dimensional crafts.

About the Book

Papercrafting needn't just mean creating two-dimensional items such as cards and scrapbook pages. In the sections that follow, you will find a variety of wonderful three-dimensional projects for every occasion, using simple and easily mastered paper-sculpting techniques. If you are a novice paper sculptor, you will be transported back to your school days as you use half-forgotten skills to fold, bend, curve, curl, pleat and stitch paper into the most fantastic shapes and creations. And experienced papercrafters will be delighted by this opportunity to extend their skills to embrace new, exciting and satisfying techniques.

A clever formation of scores and folds creates a 3D diamond pattern in a band of gold card to add sophistication and distinction to a dressing-up crown.

The base and lid of this fun gift box are made by curving and gluing a card strip with a folded tabbed edge to a circle, then decorated with cone cherries and a rolled-paper candle.

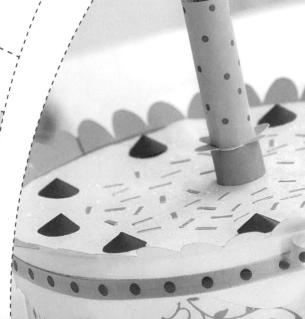

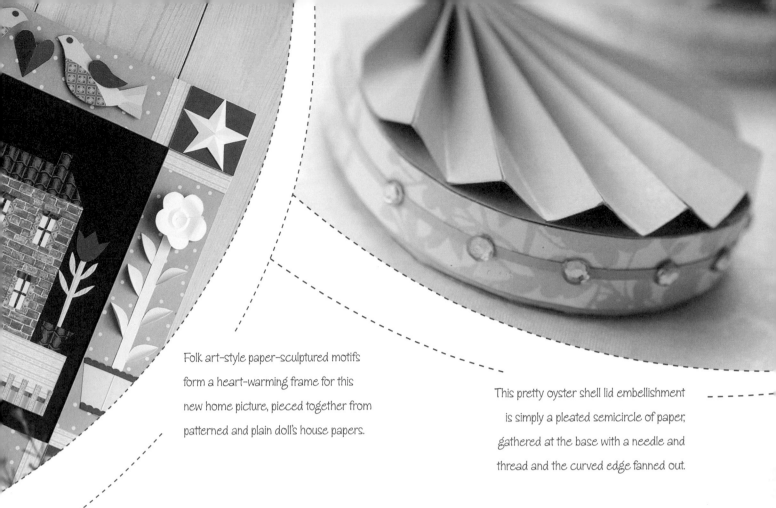

Folk art-style paper-sculptured motifs form a heart-warming frame for this new home picture, pieced together from patterned and plain doll's house papers.

This pretty oyster shell lid embellishment is simply a pleated semicircle of paper, gathered at the base with a needle and thread and the curved edge fanned out.

In the end section (see pages 94–103), you will find a step-by-step guide to all the core paper-sculpting techniques, along with practical advice on choosing and using the required tools and papers. You can then apply these skills to making any of the projects you choose. For instance, with simple scoring and folding you can create a fabulous 3D frame for a patchwork paper picture, or, with a series of folds and cuts, a decorative dimensional band for a king's crown; curl strips of patterned paper to form a flamboyant chrysanthemum bloom, or pleat pearlized card to replicate an oyster shell for a dainty gift box; curve paper into a cone shape to make an elegant teacup, or card into a sided circular shape for a novelty birthday cake gift box. And why not use stitching to add convincing detail to a handbag gift bag? All the templates you need to create these intriguing items are provided at the back of the book (see pages 105–119).

Your Future in 3D!

What's most important is to enjoy learning these new, highly versatile techniques and using them in all their creative applications. After a while, you'll find yourself looking at everyday objects in an entirely fresh way and wondering how you can re-create them from paper. At this point it will be time to set off on your own path with the confidence to design and personalize your own three-dimensional projects to make gifts, mementoes and keepsakes that will delight your family and friends.

Sweet Cupcakes

Cupcakes are all the rage, and these pretty versions make a sweet treat for Mother's Day or a special birthday. Made from pastel-coloured papers, they look stunning on their own or en masse in a handmade presentation box. Each cake hides a secret; the lid lifts off to reveal a little message, an invitation or a special thought.

The basic cupcake design can be easily adapted for other celebrations. For a wedding, make the cakes from white paper with silver cases and scatter the tops with pink paper rosebuds. Alternatively, welcome a new baby into the world with a dainty cupcake dusted with tiny punched flowers, or add a fun cupcake covered with silver foil baubles and glitter 'icing' to a little girl's party bags. Also great for entertaining children are the bunny cupcakes on page 11 – the perfect Easter gift!

A single cupcake looks sumptuously inviting nestling in a colour-coordinated gift box – see page 102 for how to make this lidded baker's-style box. For an alternative flower centre, simply form a contrasting-coloured paper circle into a cone (see page 99).

Floral Cupcake

The cupcakes are constructed on a circular base with tabbed sides (see page 100). A strip of paper with scalloped edges is wrapped around the base to create a shallow wall that will keep the top of the cake in place. The cake top is a cone shape, with a flower added to form a handle. Crimped card is ideal for making a highly realistic pleated cake case, but if you are short of time, you could use real cake or muffin cases, which are available in a variety of colours.

You will need:

- medium-weight paper in pastel shades of pink, orange, blue and yellow

- pastel-coloured crimped card

- small label

- basic tool kit (see pages 94–95)

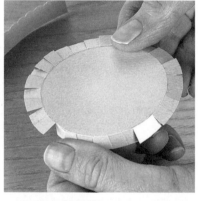

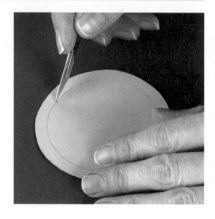

1 To make the cupcake cut a cupcake base from pastel pink paper using the template on page 105. Score and crease around the inner circle where marked on the template.

2 Snip at evenly spaced intervals around the base, from the outer edge to the inner scored circle, to make tabs. Fold the tabs under (see page 100).

3 Cut a 1.5 x 22cm (⅝ x 8½in) strip of pastel orange paper. Gently curl by pulling it over the closed blades of your scissors (see page 99). Cut along one long edge with scallop-edged scissors. Stick a length of narrow double-sided tape to the wrong side of the strip, then wrap the strip around the base, covering the tabs.

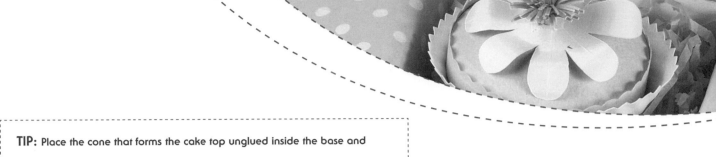

TIP: Place the cone that forms the cake top unglued inside the base and overlap the edges until you achieve a perfect fit before sticking them together.

4 Cut a cupcake top from pastel blue paper using the template on page 105. Snip from the edge to the centre where marked, then overlap the cut edges to make a cone that sits perfectly on the base (see page 99). Stick the overlapped edges together with double-sided tape.

5 **To make the flower,** use a pair of compasses to draw a 6cm (2⅜in) circle on to pastel yellow paper and cut out. Fold the paper in half, then into quarters and finally into eighths.

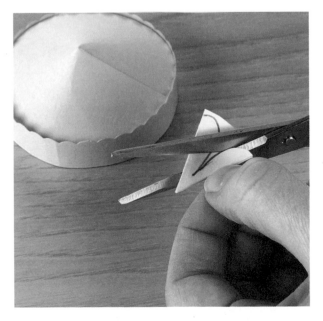

6 Using a pencil, draw a half petal adjoining each of the two folded edges, as shown. Carefully snip around the pencil lines, taking care not to cut through the folded edges.

7 Unfold the paper to reveal the flower. Curl each petal in turn by pulling it over the closed blades of your scissors, as in Step 3.

8 Cut a 2cm (¾in) wide strip of pastel orange paper to make the stamens. Draw a faint line 5mm (¼in) from one long edge. Snip along the strip, making very narrow cuts, up to the pencil line. Tightly roll the strip and stick the ends together with double-sided tape. Fan out the stamens, then glue to the centre of the flower.

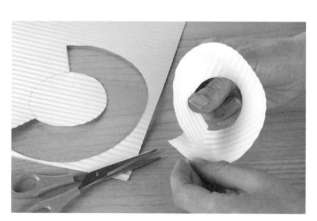

9 **Cut a paper case** from crimped card using the template on page 105. Trim the upper edge with zigzag scissors. Tape the short edges together to measure approximately 8cm (3⅛in) across.

10 **To finish,** run a thin line of PVA (white) glue around the lower edge of the cake base. Place the cake gently in the case and make sure that it sits straight. Leave to dry. Write a message on a small label and place inside the cake.

Bunny Cupcakes

Children will be delighted by these cheeky Easter Bunny cupcakes that conceal a nest of delicious chocolate treats. It is easy to vary the design to create a range of animals simply by changing the colour and style of the ears. Try cutting a round nose and shorter ears from pink paper for a pig, or short, pointed ears for a cat.

You will need:

- pastel pink, bright green and brown medium-weight paper

- pastel-coloured crimped card

- scraps of blue, pink and white lightweight paper

- basic tool kit (see pages 94–95)

1 **To make the basic cupcake,** follow Steps 1–4 on pages 8–9, cutting the side from bright green paper and the top from brown paper. Use zigzag scissors to cut the upper edge of the green paper to resemble grass. Punch two dots from blue paper for eyes and cut the nose and mouth from pink paper. Cut the ears from brown paper and ear insides from pink paper using the templates on page 105, then glue together. Score and turn under the ears where marked. Curl the ears by pulling over the closed blades of your scissors. Glue to the top of the head.

2 Cut the whiskers from white lightweight paper using the template on page 105, then glue to the bunny's face, on either side of its nose.

Pretty Pictures

The design for this unique new home gift is inspired by American and European folk art, in which plain and patterned fabrics are blended together in patchwork. But here a similar effect has been produced using patterned and plain doll's house papers, combining wallpaper, brick and tile patterns to create a house and garden framed by a border of traditional motifs in 3D form.

You could easily personalize the picture by adding a message or names and dates below the house, or reduce the house template and use to make a new home card. For an alternative design for children, trace an image of a fairy castle from a book or magazine, then use iridescent papers to build up the elements. The frame motifs could be hearts and crowns or tiaras (see page 41).

These well-loved, homely motifs not only complement the main picture by adding to its warm welcome but their sculptured forms contribute an intriguing sense of depth and drama, and draw the eye unerringly to the house.

New Home Picture

The picture and frame are cut from heavy mount board, which makes a perfectly smooth, flat surface to work on, and a dark blue colour chosen to accentuate the patterns and tones in the papers. The house and garden are glued to scraps of mount board to raise them above the background, while the border motifs have been made three-dimensional by the use of paper-sculpture techniques.

2 Roughly cut a lawn, roof, house, door and door panels from doll's house papers using the templates on pages 106–107. Cut out the house windows and doorway. Glue the components to the scraps of mount board, then cut out neatly. Cut the wall from stone paper using the template on page 107 and glue to the lawn.

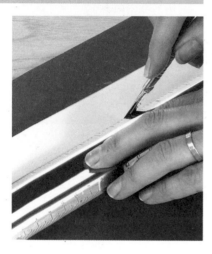

1 For the picture cut a 30cm (12in) square of blue mount board. Use high-tack PVA (white) glue to attach it to the foam board and trim to size.

3 Cut eight windows from plain green paper and eight lintels from roof tile paper using the template on page 106. Glue in place on the house.

TIP: If you can't find doll's house papers, use standard wallpaper or giftwrap with a small pattern.

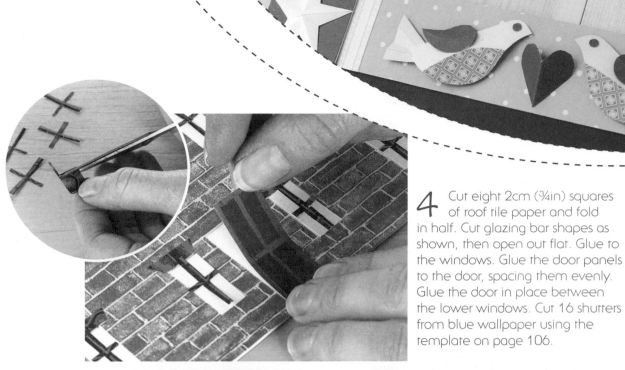

4 Cut eight 2cm (¾in) squares of roof tile paper and fold in half. Cut glazing bar shapes as shown, then open out flat. Glue to the windows. Glue the door panels to the door, spacing them evenly. Glue the door in place between the lower windows. Cut 16 shutters from blue wallpaper using the template on page 106.

5 Cut a path from blue wallpaper using the template on page 107 and glue to the middle of the lawn. Cut a 3cm (1⅛in) wide piece of striped wallpaper the same length as the lawn. Cut out alternate stripes to make a fence. Glue along the lower edge of the lawn over the wall.

6 Use high-tack PVA (white) glue to attach the house to the centre of the blue mount board square. Glue the lawn beneath, placing it centrally and lining it up exactly with the lower edge of the house. Glue the roof at the top of the house.

7 Cut two tulip pots, tulip stalks and tulip flowers from tile, wallpaper and plain red papers using the templates on page 106. Glue them at either side of the house.

8 **For the picture frame** cut a 39cm (15¼in) square of white mount board. Cut a 27cm (10½in) square from the centre to make the aperture. Glue the frame face down on to the back of the green spotted paper and trim around it.

9 Cut four 6cm (2⅜in) squares of red paper. Glue to scraps of mount board and cut them out. Glue one at each corner of the frame.

> **TIP:** You will need to change the blade in your craft knife frequently when cutting mount board, as it will blunt very quickly.

10 Cut eight strips of green wallpaper 6 x 1.5cm (2⅜ x ⅝in). Glue them to the frame either side of the red squares.

11 Cut four corner stars from white paper using the template on page 107. Score and crease them on the front and back where indicated to make them three-dimensional. Use high-tack PVA (white) glue to attach one at each corner of the picture frame.

12 Cut two flowers from yellow paper using the template on page 107. Snip along the cut line, and score and crease them on the front and back where marked to make three-dimensional. Overlap the cut edges of the flowers and glue them together.

13 Cut two flower stalks, twelve leaves and two flower pots from plain papers using the templates on page 107. Score and crease the leaves on the back where marked. Cut two strips of red paper for the top and bottom of each pot, using scallop-edged scissors to cut the top edge, and glue them to the pots. Glue the stalks, leaves and pots in place, then attach the flowers with high-tack PVA (white) glue.

14 Using the templates on page 106, cut two complete bird bodies, including tails, from plain blue paper, then reverse and cut out another two bird bodies. Repeat for the bird fronts, cutting them from blue wallpaper, and bird wings, cutting from plain red paper. Cut two hearts from plain red paper. Score and crease the bird wings and hearts where marked. Glue the bird fronts to their bodies, then score and crease the bodies and tails. Using a single-hole punch, punch dots from red paper and glue to the birds' heads as eyes. Glue the wings in place. Glue the birds and hearts to the frame.

TIP: For an especially personal touch, take a photo of the recipient's new house and garden and copy its look and style.

15 **To assemble** glue the frame to the picture with high-tack PVA (white) glue, making sure that the picture sits square within the aperture. Attach the hangers to the frame back, then thread through and tie a length of cord for hanging.

Fantasy Fairies

This flirty little fairy with her come-hither look will make a memorable present for the one you love on Valentine's Day. And having pipe-cleaner arms and legs, the recipient can have great fun posing her as he desires! Packaged in a sumptuous presentation box, she wears a glamorous evening dress with matching long gloves, but the addition of boots gives her a distinctly trendy appeal.

Alternatively, with a flowing frock of icy blue trimmed with purple, and crown, boots and gloves to match, she can be transformed into a festive fairy queen (see page 23), or dress her in floor-length traditional white and gold to make a perfect Christmas angel. A tweenie would love a miniature version of herself for a birthday, sporting a patterned paper ra-ra skirt, long-sleeved top and paper hands, or other appropriate clothing.

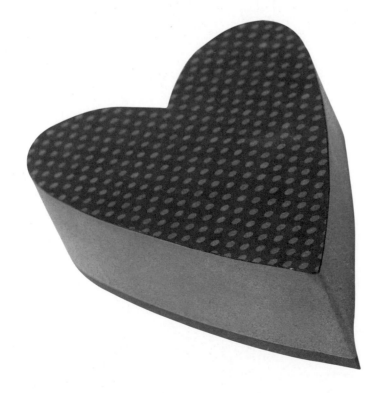

The traditional Valentine's gift package of a kitschy, heart-shaped box conceals within it, in a frothy mass of shredded pink tissue paper, an unexpected item — a suitably seductive fairy, dressed to kill! You could sprinkle in a few luxuriously wrapped chocolates beside her for good measure.

Flirty Fairy

The fairy is made from papier mâché formed around a frame of pipe cleaners. The box is constructed using the tabbed-wall technique (see page 100), with the rim of the lid fitting around the heart-shaped lid flush with the edge, whereas the rim of the box base sits about 5mm (¼in) in from the heart-shaped base. You don't need to be precise with this measurement, but just make sure that you allow enough of a lip around the base for the lid to fit over it.

1 To make the fairy twist a loop in the middle of a pipe cleaner to form her head. Point the ends of the pipe cleaner down. Twist on a second pipe cleaner just below the head to make arms. Twist on a third pipe cleaner below that to make legs. Dip the newspaper strips in PVA (white) glue diluted 60/40 with water and apply three layers around the body. Leave to dry.

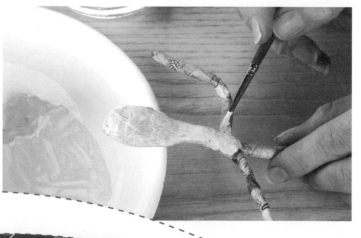

2 When the body is dry, sand the paper down to remove any rough edges. Apply two thin coats of white paint to cover up the newspaper, then leave to dry.

> **TIP:** Once you have covered the pipe-cleaner frame in papier mâché, leave in a warm place such as an airing cupboard, in the sun or by a radiator to dry overnight.

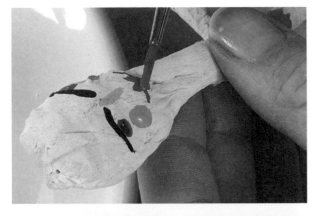

3 Lightly draw on the fairy's features and use a thin, fine paintbrush to paint them in. Paint on a little dress bodice with red paint.

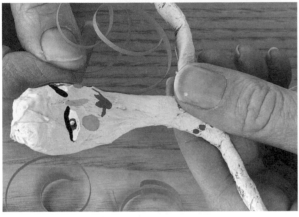

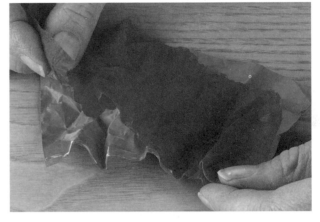

4 Cut narrow strips of pink lightweight paper and curl them over the closed blades of a pair of scissors to make the fairy's hair (see page 99). Glue the hair around the fairy's head. Add very short, straight pieces at the front to make her fringe.

5 Cut a 6cm (2⅜in) wide strip of pink lightweight paper for the skirt. Crumple the paper, then open it out and attach a piece of double-sided tape to the back top edge. Crumple a slightly shorter piece of red tissue paper and glue it along the top of the skirt front. Tightly gather the top and stick around the fairy's waist.

> **TIP:** The fairy's skirt may seem very wide for such a narrow waist, but you need to crumple it up firmly, then gather the waist to the right size to make it as full as possible before you stick it in place.

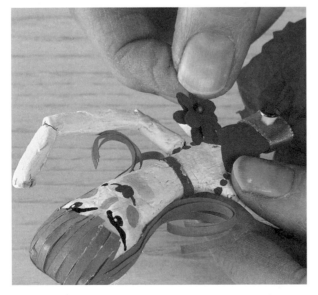

6 Glue a length of pink narrow ribbon around the top of the skirt. Glue a red gem stone on top. Glue a narrow strip of red lightweight paper around the fairy's neck, then attach a fabric flower on top with an adhesive foam pad.

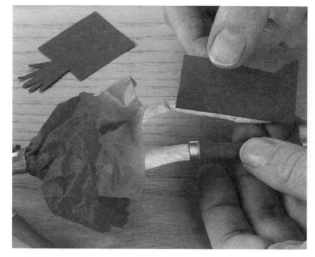

7 Cut two boots and gloves from red lightweight paper using the templates on page 108. Run a line of glue along the straight edge of each boot, roll around the fairy's legs so that the feet end up at the front and stick in place. Position the gloves so that the hands sit at the ends of her arms. Apply glue along one edge of the upper part of each glove, roll around her arms and stick in place. Add narrow strips of gold lightweight paper to the gloves and boots.

8 Cut two wings and a heart from gold lightweight card using the templates on page 108. Score and crease where marked. Attach the heart to a length of thin wire to make a wand. Glue the wings to the fairy's back.

9 **To make the box** cut a box base and lid from red medium-weight card using the template on page 108. For the box rims, cut two 6.5 x 75cm (2½ x 29½in) lengths of red card, then score and crease a 1.5cm (⅝in) border down one long side of each. Snip along the borders, then glue one rim around the base 5mm (¼in) in from the edge of the heart, and one to the lid flush with the edge of the heart (see page 100).

10 Place the lid face down on the sheet of red patterned paper and draw around it. Cut out the paper and glue to the lid. Fill the box with a layer of pink shredded tissue paper, then place the fairy inside.

Festive Fairy

This wintery-styled version of the fairy with her delicately coloured dress and accessories makes a striking, contemporary decoration for Christmas time. The boots and gloves are made as for the Flirty Fairy. The dress is a long rectangle of thick tissue paper, trimmed with self-adhesive satin ribbon, then crumpled and opened out again. The top is gathered and glued around the fairy's neck and a slit cut in either side for her arms. It is finished off with a brooch formed from two buttons glued together. A snowflake punched from white paper decorates her wand. The delicate crown is made from wire threaded with tiny beads and sequins, with the additional flourish of a beaded plume recycled from a Christmas decoration.

Oyster Shell

For a really special keepsake for a teenage girl, this charming gift box is sure to be treasured. The box is simple, yet decorative enough to give as an alternative to a card. It also makes an ideal little jewellery box for holding small items, such as bracelets or earrings. The design is based on vintage powder compacts of the 1920s and 30s, and has a distinctive air of elegance. Restrained, retro-style papers have been chosen for the box to make it quite naturalistic in colour.

This dainty box can be used in so many ways. Apart from holding jewellery, it would also make a stylish container for other personal treasures, such as a mini bottle of your favourite scent, a single deluxe chocolate or simply a little handwritten birthday message. Made in pastel shades, it could hold a lock of baby hair, or use dark red or shocking pink to create a striking Valentine's gift box.

Deceptively easy to make, this little box is full of understated style and sophistication, with its oyster shell lid of neatly pleated pearlized card and jewel-studded rim.

Oyster Shell

The box lid and base are made using a tabbed-wall construction (see page 100). A semicircle of paper always forms a perfect shell shape when you pleat it carefully, and it can be done in minutes with satisfying results. Subtly patterned paper and light-catching diamante stones embellish the box lid, while patterned papers line the inside.

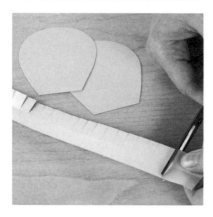

1 **To create the box** cut a box base and lid from pearlized lilac lightweight card using the template on page 108. Cut two 2.5 x 28cm (1 x 11in) strips of lilac card and score and fold them 1cm (⅜in) below the top edge. Snip along the strips at evenly spaced intervals halfway across their width to make tabs.

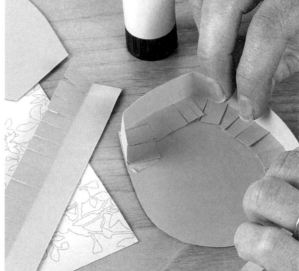

2 Fold the tabs under. Using a glue stick, glue one strip around the base of the shell and the other around the lid to make rims (see page 100). Cover the lid rim with a strip of pearlized patterned paper.

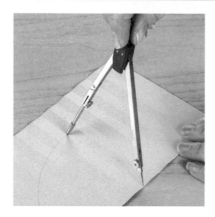

3 **To make the shell** score a 20 x 10cm (8 x 4in) piece of lilac card every 2cm (¾in) on the front and back, alternating the score lines to fold the paper every 1cm (⅜in) concertina-style (see page 100). Pleat the paper, then lay flat. Using a pair of compasses, draw a semicircle with a radius of 8.5cm (3⅜in) on to the card.

4 Cut out the semicircle, then re-pleat it to make a shell shape. Press the sides of the shell firmly together. Place the shell on a cutting mat and pierce a hole in the base from front to back through all the layers using a bradawl or darning needle.

TIP: Open and shut the concertina folds of the shell several times so that it retains its shape when you attach it to the top of the lid.

5 Stitch through the holes with strong thread. Pull the thread firmly and knot it tightly under the shell to keep the edges together.

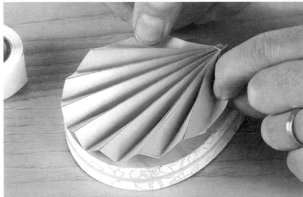

6 Once the shell is firmly stitched, gently fan out the shape so that it fits the box lid. Cover the top of the lid with strips of double-sided tape. Fan out the shell so that it completely covers the lid and press it gently on to the tape to keep it in place.

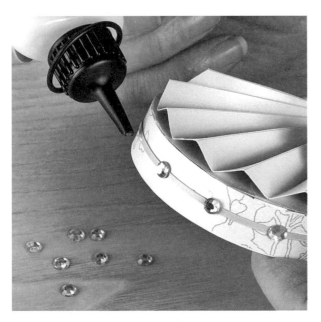

7 To finish, cut a box base and lid from the patterned paper using the template on page 108. Glue them to the inside of the box and lid to cover the tabs. Cut a narrow strip of the lilac card 28cm (11cm) in length and glue centrally around the rim of the lid. Use high-tack PVA (white) glue to stick diamante jewels at evenly spaced intervals along the lilac strip.

Fabulous Frames

A golden wedding is a real milestone, and what could be more fitting than an ornamental 3D frame to complement a photo of the event – a wedding-day shot of the golden couple or perhaps a black and white picture of the venue. Inspired by wedding cake icing designs, the frame features traditional motifs entirely sculptured in white paper.

The number can be changed to tie in with any other wedding anniversary, and related elements worked into the design, such as touches of silver for a 25th or ruby-coloured 3D diamond motifs (see pages 66–70) for a 40th. Or for a wedding gift, you could echo the particular icing scheme of the couple's cake in your frame motifs. The same principles can be adapted to make a dainty baby or child's photo frame decorated with pastel-coloured daisies and 3D leaves and hearts (see pages 34–35).

Hearts and entwined rings are powerful symbols of love and marriage, but also make a striking visual impact in their sculptured 3D forms. The frame also features curved foliage for a carved, architectural feel – architectural pattern books offer a good source of motifs.

You will need:

- A2 (16½ x 23⅜in) sheet of 5mm (¼in) thick foam board

- A3 (12 x 16½in) sheet of white lightweight card

- A2 (16½ x 23⅜in) sheet of heavyweight watercolour paper

- small flower punch

- basic tool kit (see pages 94–95)

A Special Anniversary

The frame is made from foam board, which is strong yet very light and easy to cut with a craft knife. The various motifs are cut from heavyweight watercolour paper, then simply scored and creased to make them three-dimensional. They can be attached with either PVA (white) glue or with adhesive foam pads. By keeping the whole design in plain white, the essential form and structure of the frame and its decorative detail have been given extra emphasis.

2 Cut the spacers and backing board from foam board using the templates on page 109. Glue the spacers to the backing board, then glue the backing board to the back of the frame aligning with the aperture, with the open side at the top.

1 To make the frame base cut the frame from foam board and also the frame top from white lightweight card using the templates on pages 109–110 – use scallop-edged scissors for the curved top and zigzag scissors for the straight bottom edge. Attach the frame top to the frame with PVA (white) glue.

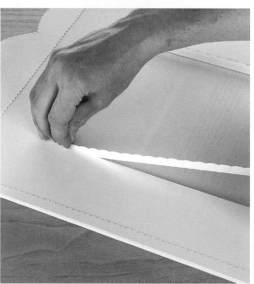

3 Use scallop-edged scissors to cut three 5mm (¼in) wide strips of watercolour paper to fit around the edges of the frame, mitring them at a 45° angle at each corner. Glue them in place, lining up the edges neatly. Cut another strip the same width to fit the inside edges of the aperture, making three right-angled bends to fit the corners. Glue in place.

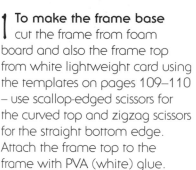

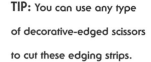

> **TIP:** You can use any type of decorative-edged scissors to cut these edging strips.

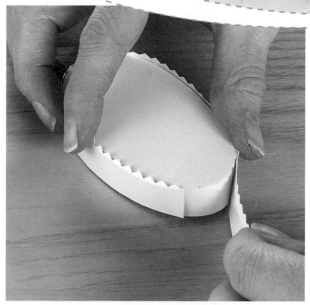

4 **For the frame motifs** cut two ovals from white lightweight card using the template on page 110. Cut two 2 x 20cm (¾ x 8in) strips of the card. Score and crease down the centre of the strips, then snip tabs along one edge. Glue each strip around the back of an oval and overlap the ends (see page 100). Trim off the excess card.

5 Cut two 1.5cm (⅝in) wide strips of watercolour paper, using zigzag scissors to cut one long edge. Glue a strip to the side of each oval, with the zigzags uppermost.

6 Cut all the curved pieces from watercolour paper using the templates on page 110. Score and crease where marked. Glue the ovals to the top and bottom of the frame, then glue the curved pieces around the ovals.

7 Cut eight rings from watercolour paper using the template on page 110. Cut, score and crease where marked. Overlap the ends of one ring and keep them in place with double-sided tape. Loop a second ring through the first, and tape the ends as before. Repeat with the remaining six rings to make four pairs. Attach a pair of rings to each corner of the frame.

8 Cut two large leaves from watercolour paper using the templates on page 110. Score and crease where marked. Use an eyelet punch and a tack hammer to make decorative holes in the lower half of each leaf (see page 95).

9 Cut six large hearts and six small hearts from watercolour paper using the templates on page 110. Score and crease where marked. Glue two large hearts at the top of the frame, with the large leaves below.

10 Using the flower punch, punch small flower shapes from watercolour paper and glue them randomly over the surface of the frame. Glue a border of punched flowers around the inside edge of each oval.

TIP: If you haven't got a small flower punch, use a small heart punch instead, or a single-hole punch to make dots.

11 Cut eight small leaves from watercolour paper using the templates on page 110. Score and crease where marked. Glue the leaves in pairs down the sides of the frame. Glue four large and four small hearts between the leaves.

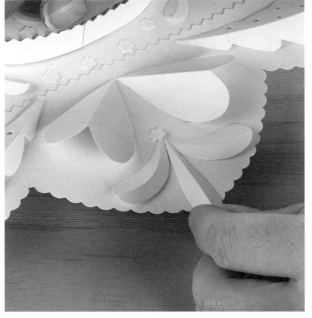

12 Cut the fleur-de-lys from watercolour paper using the template on page 110. Score and crease on the front where marked. Glue to the centre top of the frame, with a punched flower at the base.

13 Cut the numbers '5' and '0' from watercolour paper using the templates on page 110. Score and crease where marked. Glue the numbers to the top oval and the remaining two small hearts to the bottom oval.

> **TIP:** To add a couple's name to the frame, print out the names in italic script on to tracing paper, then trim the paper to match the shape of the lower oval.

Perfectly Framed

This cute photo frame, sprinkled with colourful daisies and hearts, is perfect for holding a picture of a baby or a little girl. Because the motifs are small, this project is great for using up scraps of paper, perhaps left over from another project.

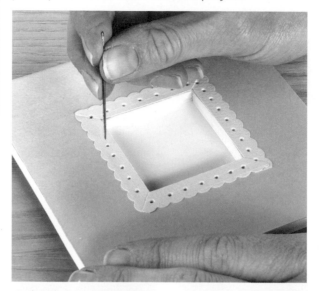

1 To make the basic frame cut the frame, spacer and backing board from foam board using the diagram on page 111. Glue the spacer and backing board to the back of the frame. Cover the frame with lilac paper. Cut the frame border from green paper, using scallop-edged scissors for the outer edge, and glue in place. Punch holes around the border with a darning needle.

2 For the decorative motifs cut 16 leaves from green paper and four hearts from pink paper using the templates on page 111. Score as instructed and crease down the centre. Glue the hearts at the corners of the border.

3 Use the daisy punch to punch four daisies from blue paper and four from yellow paper. Use a single-hole punch to make dots from orange paper and glue one in the centre of each daisy. Fold up the petals. Glue the blue daisies in the corners of the frame, with the yellow ones in between.

4 Glue the leaves beneath the daisies. Use the small flower punch to punch four small flowers from pink paper and glue one to the centre of each side of the border.

Keepsake Boxes

For a totally unique way to mark the birth of a new baby, what could be more magical than this beautiful keepsake card box? The new mother will be enchanted when she lifts off the box lid to reveal a pair of tiny shoes in their personalized decorative setting – a card they are sure to treasure even when the baby has grown up into a strapping teenager!

To adapt the design for a baby girl, simply choose pink papers instead of blue. You can also create other 3D paper items to feature in a card box to celebrate different occasions, such as a mini bouquet of flowers for Mother's Day or a simple Christmas tree and gifts for the festive season. For a wedding, see the fabulous three-tier cake idea on pages 40–41.

This beautiful box card will deliver a real wow factor when its contents are discovered by the proud parents. Add an ornamental name and date tag to personalize your card for an extra-special finishing touch. This example features a buggy motif created using three-quarters of a circle, trimmed with contrasting scallop-edged borders.

Baby Booties

The shoes are constructed over a lightweight card base. Delicately patterned scrapbooking paper has been used to form the uppers, which holds its shape well and is just the right weight for rolling and curling to make the shoes three-dimensional. Pearly, silhouette papers reminiscent of vintage lace designs have been added to the back and sides of the box.

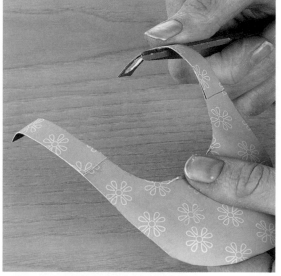

2 Using the template on page 111, cut two shoe uppers from patterned scrapbooking paper. Gently curl the sides and backs of the uppers by pulling them over the closed blades of your scissors to make them three-dimensional (see page 99).

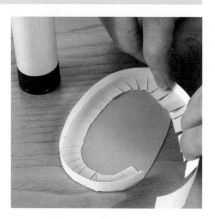

1 To make the shoes cut the soles from lightweight card using the templates on page 111. Cut two strips 1.5 x 26cm (⅝ x 10in) from card. Score each 5mm (¼in) from one long edge down the width. Snip along the strips from the other long edge up to the scored line to make tabs. Fold the tabs under. Glue one strip around each sole.

3 Spread a thin line of glue around the rims of the shoe soles. Place the uppers on the soles and overlap the backs of the shoes until the uppers sit neatly. Leave enough upper to cover the fronts of the shoes. Press them into place.

TIP: Make the box from heavy card (mount board) without a lid to create a decorative box frame to hang on the wall – simply attach two self-adhesive hangers and thin cord to the back.

4 Cut two insoles from contrasting scrapbooking paper using the template on page 111, reversing one. Glue in place. Snip the fronts of the uppers. Curve down to cover the sole front rim. Cut a 5mm (¼in) wide strip and glue around the outside of each shoe, aligning with the lower edge.

5 Cut two 7mm (¼in) wide strips of the same paper to make straps. Curl the paper with scissors, as in Step 2, then glue in place, covering the end of each strap with a button. Cut two lengths of ric-rac braid and glue one around the outside of each shoe, just above the lower edge.

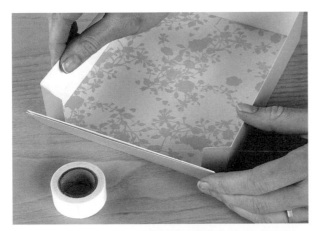

6 **To make the box** follow Steps 1–2 on page 102 to cut the box and lid from blue medium-weight card and score. Cut two pieces of patterned paper, one to cover the bottom of the box and the other the inside of the box lid, and glue in place. Follow Steps 2–3 on page 102 to complete the box and lid. Cover the sides of the box and lid inside and top with contrasting patterned papers.

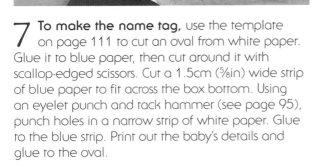

7 **To make the name tag,** use the template on page 111 to cut an oval from white paper. Glue it to blue paper, then cut around it with scallop-edged scissors. Cut a 1.5cm (⅝in) wide strip of blue paper to fit across the box bottom. Using an eyelet punch and tack hammer (see page 95), punch holes in a narrow strip of white paper. Glue to the blue strip. Print out the baby's details and glue to the oval.

8 **To finish,** glue the name tag to the box bottom, about 4cm (1½in) up from the lower edge. Stick double-sided tape to the back of each shoe and attach to the box bottom, above the name tag. Add the lid.

You will need:

- A4 (US Letter) sheet of white lightweight card

- scraps of black medium-weight paper

- A3 (12 x 16½in) sheet of pink medium-weight card

- A3 (12 x 16½in) sheet of lace-effect wedding giftwrap

- 2 x A4 (US Letter) sheets of patterned paper

- A4 (US Letter) sheet of white tissue paper

- scraps of gold and pink paper

- diamante jewels

- heart punch

- basic tool kit (see pages 94–95)

Wedding Day

Celebrate the wedding of friends or family with this beautiful box card. The couple's names and the wedding date are added to a three-tier cake for a fun memento of their special day. Pretty lace-effect wedding giftwrap is used to cover the box and accessories added to mark the occasion, such as a white tissue paper veil, a tiara (template on page 112) enriched with diamante jewels and a gold punched heart to crown the cake. Follow Step 6 on page 39 to make up the basic box and lid.

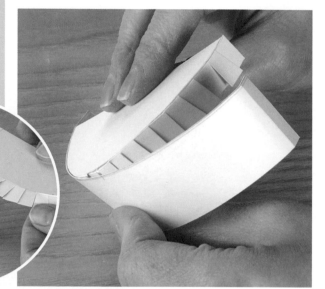

1 **To make the cake** cut the three tiers from white lightweight card using the templates on page 112. Score and snip where marked, then fold the tabs under. Spread glue along one long edge of each tier and curve it around the cake top, covering the tabs (see page 100). Glue together, then glue the cake to the box bottom.

2 **To make the hat** cut all the hat pieces from black paper using the templates on page 112, scoring and snipping where marked. Glue the edges of the hat together and fan out the tabs. Slide the hat brim over the hat and glue it in place.

3 Fold down the tabs of the hat crown and spread a little glue on them. Insert the crown into the top of the hat. Before you glue the hat inside the box, snip the back of the brim flush with the hat so that it will sit flat against the box bottom.

Piece of Cake

Gift boxes make a great alternative to giftwrap, especially if you are looking for a novel way to present a gift or have lots of little offerings. This birthday cake box is suitable for adults or children, and comes complete with icing, glacé cherries and a sprinkling of hundreds and thousands. It even has a candle, a single larger-than-life version, although you could add as many as you like to reflect the recipient's age.

There are so many ways to adapt this design. Simply changing the colour scheme to lilac or yellow would make it ideal for a baby's first birthday, or make it in white, perhaps with an extra tier, to transform it into a wedding cake. A chocolate or coffee cake, in dark or light brown card, would be perfect for Father's Day.

This inviting, realistic-looking cake box is just right for packaging a special, non-bulky item of clothing in an unexpected way, such as a blouse, shirt or T-shirt, or use it as a creative way of presenting several small wrapped gifts. Alternatively, for a single, small item such as a piece of jewellery, opt for the one-slice variation on page 47.

Birthday Cake

The basic box is made from lightweight oiled stencil card, which is highly flexible yet very strong. The top and sides are covered with pretty frosted papers that would be too flimsy to use on their own. A ring of cherries decorates the top, made from small, flat cones of red paper; for extra sparkle, try making silver balls from rolled aluminium foil. Pastel colours that complement the cake were chosen for the candle.

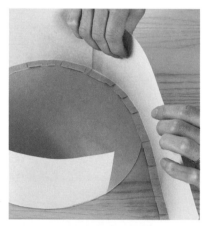

1 **For the box base,** using a pair of compasses, draw a 23cm (9in) diameter circle on to the stencil card. Cut a 23 x 75cm (9 x 29½in) strip of the same card (cut and glue together two strips to make up the required length). Score and crease a 1cm (⅜in) border along one long edge of the strip. Snip tabs along the border, then glue the strip around the circle (see page 100).

2 Draw a 22.5cm (8⅞in) circle on to stencil card and cut out. Glue the circle inside the box, covering the base.

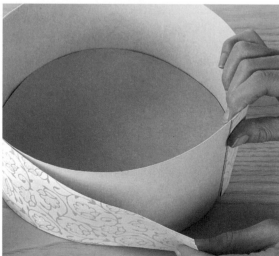

3 Cut a strip of pink patterned paper 10 x 80cm (4 x 31½in) (again, cut and glue together two strips to make up the required length). Glue it around the box base to cover the card, overlapping the ends.

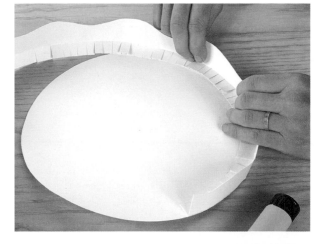

4 **For the box lid,** cut a 23.5cm (9¼in) diameter circle from white medium-weight card. Cut a 6.5 x 80cm (2½ x 31½in) wide strip of the same white card (again, glue together two strips). Score and crease a 1cm (⅜in) border along one long edge of the strip. Draw a wavy edge along the other long edge of the strip and cut it out. Snip along the border and glue the strip around the circle of card.

> **TIP:** Where the card and paper pieces have to be joined, make sure that the joins all line up at the back to make them as inconspicuous as possible.

5 Cut a 23cm (9in) circle from white medium-weight card and glue to the inside of the lid. Cut a 23.5cm (9¼in) circle from the other pink patterned paper to cover the lid top. Glue in place.

6 Cut a scallop-edged border from plain pink paper to fit around the lid using the template on page 113 (glue two pieces together to make up the required length of 80cm/31½in). Score and crease the border where marked. Attach the border around the lid with glue.

> **TIP:** Paper that has been curved tends to spring back into shape before the glue has dried, so if you are experiencing problems, use narrow double-sided tape to attach the pink border around the top of the cake.

7 **For the cherries,** cut nine cherries from red paper using the template on page 113. Snip each cherry to the centre, as marked, then curve round the edges to make small cones (see page 99). Glue the cherries in a ring around the lid.

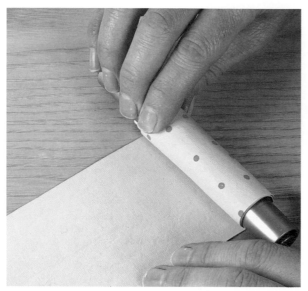

8 **For the candle,** cut an 8 x 10cm (3⅛ x 4in) strip of blue spotted paper. Roll the paper around a marker pen to make a tube and stick the ends in place with double-sided tape. Slip the tube off the pencil.

9 Cut out the candle holder from pink patterned paper using the template on page 113. Score and crease where marked. Glue it around the base of the candle, about 1cm (⅜in) from the end, overlapping the ends and trimming to fit.

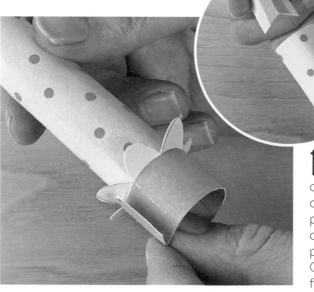

10 Cut a 1.5cm (⅝in) wide strip of plain pink paper and glue it around the base of the candle holder. Using the template on page 113, cut the whole candle flame shape from yellow paper, then cut around the middle solid line from orange paper and the inner solid line from plain pink paper. Score and crease where marked. Glue the flame layers together, then glue the flame inside the top of the candle.

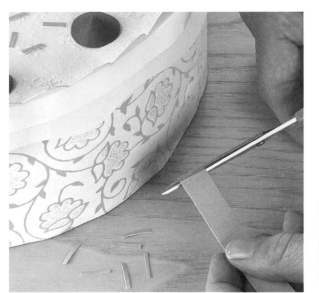

11 Glue the candle to the top of the cake. Snip 1cm (⅜in) wide strips of plain pink paper for hundreds and thousands. Glue them to the top of the cake. Wrap a length of pink spotted narrow ribbon around the box lid and tie in a bow. Glue pink ric-rac braid around the base of the box.

TIP: To personalize the box, write a name or message on the top of the cake with dimensional glue and it will look just like icing!

Single Slice

This one-slice cake box variation is constructed in exactly the same way as the large box, but using a one-sixth section of the template. The rim of the lid is extended in depth so that it completely covers the sides of the box. To create the effect of a cream and jam filling, a narrow strip of white paper has been glued to the long sides of the box, then a slightly narrower strip of red paper glued on top. Instead of a candle holder, the candle has been wrapped with a narrow strip of gold paper.

Gorgeous Garlands

Simple paper shapes make the most unexpected forms if they are joined together in multiples. Here, hearts cut from plain and coloured vellum paper are glued together in sets of six, then inverted to make teardrop shapes, which look lovely strung into a delicate garland. Semicircles cut from decorative Japanese papers are again joined in groups of six to create stylized flower-like forms or something reminiscent of star anise spice. These have pale pink and blue pearl beads added for a touch of glamour.

Also featured on pages 52–53 are folded circles used to create glorious globes – you may perhaps have made decorations like these at school. Reproduced in pretty pastel or translucent papers, the results can be stunning, especially when suspended in groups from the ceiling at different heights.

These snazzy baubles are made in exactly the same way as the teardrop and semicircle decorations (see pages 50–51), but in this case six circles, folded down the centre, have been glued together. This is a great opportunity to give leftover Christmas giftwrap a new lease of life – it's just too valuable to waste!

Teardrops

Vellum is great to work with, as it creases beautifully and is stiff enough to hold its shape. After the six folded vellum hearts have been glued together, a short metal eye pin (used in jewellery making) is inserted down the centre and the end formed into a loop with pliers to keep it in place. Eye pins can be found in most bead shops and some craft retailers, or order them online.

1 To make the multiple shapes cut six hearts from the sheets of vellum paper, folded in half with the centre of the heart placed along the fold, using the template on page 113.

2 To assemble the shapes place five of the hearts side by side, then butt up against each other and glue the adjacent halves of the hearts together.

3 Add the sixth heart, gluing one half to the fifth heart and one half to the first heart to complete the shape. Press all the joined sides together firmly.

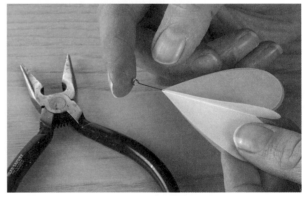

4 To add the wire hanger take an eye pin and push it carefully down the centre of the decoration until the eye rests on the top of the shape. Using pliers, twist the other end of the pin into a loop to keep it in place. Make several of the decorations and thread on to a length of embroidery silk or thin wire to make a garland.

TIP: These decorations look good hung either way up; when hung the other way up, they are more recognizable as hearts.

Semicircles

Although six semicircles have been joined together here, you can use a larger quantity to make a much more complex shape. As with the teardrop decorations, eye pins have been inserted through the decorations so that they can be strung together to make a garland, but here the pins have been threaded with some small pearly beads in colours to coordinate with the papers.

You will need:

- A4 (US Letter) sheets of handmade patterned papers in pale colours

- large and small pale pink and blue pearl beads

- metal eye pins

- embroidery silk or thin wire

- pliers

- basic tool kit (see pages 94–95)

1 **To make the multiple shapes,** using a pair of compasses, draw three 6cm (2⅜in) diameter circles on to the paper. Cut out the circles and fold them in half.

2 Fold each semicircle in half again so that you have six folded semicircles.

3 **To assemble the shapes** butt five of the semicircles up against each other and glue together. Add the sixth semicircle, gluing one half to the fifth semicircle and one half to the first to complete the shape. Press all the joined sides together firmly.

4 **To add the wire hanger** thread a large and small bead on to an eye pin. Push the pin down through the decoration and thread another bead on to the end. Twist the end of the wire into a loop to keep the pin in place. Make several of the decorations and thread on to a length of embroidery silk or thin wire to make a garland.

TIP: Instead of creating a garland, you could make these dainty decorations into a pair of earrings by threading them on to earring hooks or studs, available from jewellery suppliers.

Globes

It's simpler to make the globes in small sections first, then join them together, otherwise you can lose track of the shape and add too many circles! You will need three domed sections, each with five joined circles and five single circles. Once the domes are joined and you have three-quarters of your basic shape, it will be easy to see where the five remaining circles slot in.

1 **To create the multiple shapes,** using a pair of compasses, draw 20 circles with a diameter of 8cm (3⅛in) on to the paper (you will get six circles out of one sheet of A4/US Letter paper). Cut out a triangle from lightweight card using the template on page 113. Place the triangle in the centre of each circle and lightly draw around with a pencil to make score lines. Score along the lines.

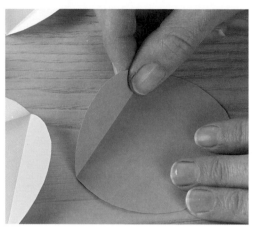

2 Lay the circles flat, scored-side down, and gently fold up the flaps.

3 **To assemble the shapes** place two circles side by side and glue the flaps together, matching them as nearly as possible. Continue to join the circles together until you have a group of five. Add the fifth circle, gluing it to the first and fourth circles, to make a dome. Make two more domes.

> **TIP:** If the edges of the circles don't quite match when you glue them together, trim them carefully with sharp scissors to neaten them.

4 Peg the three domes together to make three-quarters of a globe, then glue, matching the edges exactly. Add the remaining circles, one at a time, to complete the globe. Pierce a hole through the top circle with a darning needle and tie a length of thin transparent cord through to make a hanger. Alternatively, several globes can be threaded on to the cord to make a garland.

Funky Jewellery

Japanese origami techniques create such elegant shapes, such as the classic cubic water bomb, which is used here in multiples of the same size and colour as a bead to form an unusual, elegant necklace. No complicated cutting or scoring is involved in making these paper cubes, just simple folding, and they magically become three-dimensional by blowing into them!

Metallic papers give the necklace a sophisticated, adult appeal, but the cubes could easily be made more child-friendly by using plain, candy-coloured papers or fun patterned papers in any size you want. You can purchase origami papers in a variety of colours, which is the required thickness and conveniently ready-cut into squares. It's easy to get children involved in making their own necklaces – they will soon be able to master the technique and will love inflating the cubes.

Transform two bronze water bomb beads into eye-catching earrings. For each earring, cut two gold lightweight card circles by drawing around a small coin. Form a loop in the end of a 10cm (4in) length of jewellery wire. Sandwich the wire between the gold discs, pass the free end through the water bomb, then make a loop at the top and trim. Attach an earring hook to the loop, then glue a heart punched from bronze paper either side of the disc.

You will need:

- A4 (US Letter) sheets of lightweight metallic paper, 2 gold, 1 bronze and 1 silver

- scrap of gold lightweight card

- copper wire

- necklace fastener

- small coin

- pliers

- heart punch

- basic tool kit (see pages 94–95)

Origami Necklace

These cubes are made from gold metallic paper, cut into 10cm (4in) squares – the paper needs to be only slightly thicker than tissue paper, as it gets harder to manipulate the more times you fold it. The secret of making a really well-defined shape is to run your thumbnail over each fold as you do it. This gives super-sharp creases and the cubes keep their shape well once they are inflated.

1 **To make the water bomb beads** cut eight 10cm (4in) squares of gold metallic paper. Fold in half, then into quarters and open out. Re-fold diagonally from top right and top left as shown. Open out the paper and lay it flat, right-side up.

2 Fold each square in half again. Push in either side of the rectangle to form a triangle. Crease the fold lines so that the triangle lies flat.

3 Place each triangle flat. Fold up each half of the triangle so that the outer corner meets the top of the triangle and crease. Turn the triangle over and fold the other side in the same way. Once the sides are folded up, you will have a small square.

4 Place each paper square flat, with the opening running vertically. Fold in the left- and right-hand corners of the square to the centre and crease. Repeat on the other side of the square.

5 Locate the opening in the top of the folded-paper form. Blow sharply into the opening to inflate into a cube. Repeat with the other forms.

6 **To make the heart disc** draw around a small coin twice on to gold lightweight card and cut out. Cut a 4cm (1½in) length of copper wire with pliers and sandwich it between the two circles with double-sided tape. Punch a heart from bronze metallic paper and stick to the circle front. Make a loop at the top of the wire and cut off the excess.

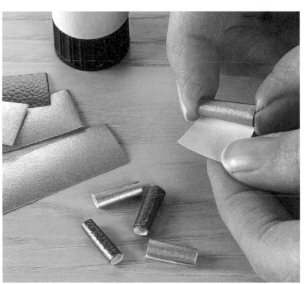

7 **To make the tubular beads** cut nine 1.5cm (⅝in) wide strips of bronze metallic paper and nine strips of silver metallic paper, cutting across the width of the sheets. Roll up and glue the ends.

8 **To assemble the necklace** cut a 50cm (20in) length of copper wire. Make a small hole in each cube on the opposite side of the opening. Thread the cubes and tubular beads on to the wire, with one silver and one bronze tubular bead between each cube. Thread the heart disc in the middle of the necklace. Attach a necklace fastener to the wire ends, then snip off the excess wire.

Glamorous Gift Bag

So many handbags, so little time! Handbags are now as desirable as shoes, so what could be more appealing to a style-loving girl than a gift bag modelled on the chic designer examples from the catwalk, made from papers in flamboyant fashion colours.

Once you have become familiar with the technique, you can adapt it to create different shapes of handbag, such as a square or rectangular bag. You can also experiment with various types of paper. Highly textural paper that has been stitched or distressed in some way is especially suitable, as it looks just like fabric. Offcuts of wallpaper are also ideal, especially if they are flocked. To make the gift bag extra personal, match the paper to the recipient's favourite pair of shoes!

The bold, flower-decorated front pocket is machine stitched to the bag with contrasting thread and provides the perfect hiding place for a small surprise gift, such as a fun item of fashion jewellery, temporary tattoos, small items of make-up or a message written on a coordinating tag.

You will need:

- A3 (12 x 16½in) sheet of brown paper
- A2 (16½ x 23⅜in) sheet of green paper
- A4 (US Letter) sheet of pink patterned paper
- scraps of plain and patterned papers
- A3 (12 x 16½in) sheet of blue patterned paper
- dark brown thread
- medium-gauge jewellery wire
- sewing machine
- daisy punch
- pliers
- sharp needle
- basic tool kit (see pages 94–95)

Handbag

The bag is made by layering different papers and stitching them together on the sewing machine (see page 101). It has a generous gusset so that more bulky gifts such as clothing and books can be easily accommodated with plenty of room for an accompanying card. A simple fastening will keep the gift safely secured inside. Punched paper shapes are threaded on to wire to make decorative handles.

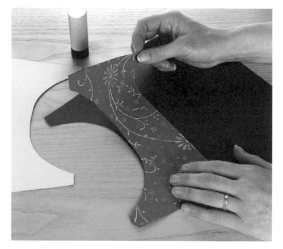

1 **To make the bag front and back** cut a handbag front from brown paper and a back from green paper using the template on page 114. Cut a front panel from pink patterned paper and glue it in place on the bag front.

2 Cut a 1cm (⅜in) wide strip of orange paper to fit along the bottom edge of the front panel. Glue the paper strip in place and then overstitch on the sewing machine using dark brown thread (see page 101).

3 Cut a pocket from green paper and the flower petals and flower centre from patterned papers using the template on page 114. Glue the flower to the pocket, then overstitch with dark brown thread. Stitch the pocket to the bag front.

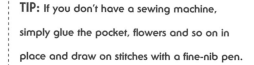

TIP: If you don't have a sewing machine, simply glue the pocket, flowers and so on in place and draw on stitches with a fine-nib pen.

4 Cut a top and side border from blue patterned paper using the handbag front/back template on page 114. Glue the strips to the bag front. Using a single-hole punch, punch a hole at the top of the bag front and back at either side for the handles.

TIP: To save on paper, use scraps of blue patterned paper for the top and side border and join them together with glue.

5 **To assemble the bag** cut a 10 x 80cm (4 x 31½in) green paper strip. Score and crease a 1cm (⅜in) wide border down each side. Snip along the borders, then curve and glue around the inside edges of the bag front and back (see page 100). Trim the excess flush with the bag top.

6 **To make the bag fastening** cut a strap from green paper using the template on page 114. Punch a daisy from brown paper, then use a pair of compasses to draw a circle to fit around the daisy on orange paper and cut out. Use a single-hole punch to punch a dot from green paper. Overstitch around the edge of the strap. Glue the dot to the daisy centre, then the daisy to the circle. Glue to the rounded end of the strap. Attach the other strap end to the bag with double-sided tape.

7 **To make the handles** cut two 50cm (20in) lengths of wire with pliers. Curve into handle shapes. Use the daisy punch and a single-hole punch to punch about 40 flowers and masses of dots from scraps of plain and patterned papers. Pierce each shape with a sharp needle and thread on to the handles, interspersing the flowers between equal blocks of dots. Thread the ends of the handles through the holes in the bag front and back, and form into small loops. Twist the free ends of the wire around the loops to close them.

Bag It Up

Here's a rarity – a gift box that appeals to men! The design of this nifty little suitcase was inspired by the smart, sturdy luggage clasped by tweedy chaps in black and white movies of yesteryear. The retro-style travel labels add to the authentic vintage look and make it ideal for a retirement voyage or a school-leaver about to embark on a gap year.

Leather-look paper has been used here to cover the suitcase, but why not experiment with other papers? There are so many fantastic scrapbooking papers available and the case would look especially good in pinstripe, houndstooth or denim paper, perhaps chosen according to the recipient's line of work to mark a promotion or new job. If you can't find suitable ready-made paper, simply colour-copy pieces of fabric to make your own.

The lid of this traditionally styled suitcase is hinged so that it opens and shuts with ease to reveal a handsomely lined interior – perfect for packaging a special book or luxuriously bound journal, a shaving or small tool kit, or a scarf or hand-knitted socks.

Suitcase

The case is constructed from foam board, as it keeps its shape much more effectively than thick card. The leather-effect paper covering the lid and base looks wonderfully convincing, but if you have trouble finding something similar, wood-effect doll's house paper makes a very good alternative. The gift box design is deliberately simple to make it easy to scale up or down. Simply alter the lid and base to the dimensions you want, then adjust the side measurements to match.

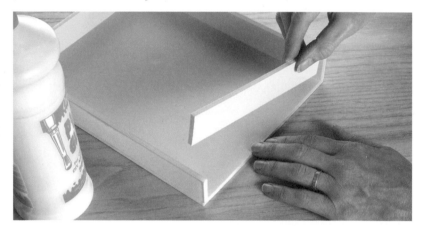

1 **For the suitcase base and lid** measure and mark them out on foam board, together with two long sides and two shorts sides, referring to the diagram on page 115. Cut them out. Lay the base and lid flat. Glue the long and short sides along the edges of the base and lid with high-tack PVA (white) glue. Leave to dry thoroughly.

2 Cut two pieces of leather-effect paper 30 x 35cm (12 x 13¾in). Place the lid and base in the centre of the paper. Fold and stick the paper over the sides of the lid and base with double-sided tape. Fold and glue the paper around the corners so that it fits neatly.

3 Cut two pieces of patterned paper 19 x 24cm (7½ x 9½in). Glue them to the inside of the base and lid. Cut 3cm (1⅛in) wide strips of dark brown paper to cover all the inside edges and glue them in place.

4 **To make the hinge** cut a piece of lightweight card 6 x 12.5cm (2⅜ x 5in). Score and crease down the centre. Place the lid and base together, then stick the hinge to the case back. Cover with a strip of leather-effect paper to neaten.

5 **For the finishing details** cut eight suitcase corners from lightweight silver card using the template on page 115. Score and crease where marked. Glue in place on the suitcase. Use a single-hole punch to punch out small dots from brown paper and glue to the corners to imitate screws.

6 Cut the handle from lightweight manila card using the template on page 115. Score and crease on the back where marked. Cover the central part of the handle with a strip of the other leather-effect paper. Make a slit in either end of the handle where marked and corresponding slits in the side of the suitcase lid. Insert split pins through the handle and lid. Cover the shanks of the pins with tape inside the lid side and conceal with a strip of paper.

7 Cut the tab from the same leather-effect paper as the handle, with a contrasting inner strip, using the template on page 115. Tape to the case front and add a Velcro dot (touch-and-close spot fastener). Cut two 1 x 27cm (⅜ x 10½in) strips of the leather-effect paper for straps. Cut and glue thinner strips of contrasting leather-effect papers to the straps. Glue a strap 2.3cm (⅞in) over the lid side and top either side of the suitcase. Cut the travel labels from coloured papers using the templates on page 116. Glue the pieces to two manila labels. Tie the Eiffel Tower label to the case handle and glue the other label to the case lid.

Capital Idea

Large capital letters make a stylish decorative feature on shelves and mantelpieces. While you can find wooden letters in junk shops, they are fairly pricey and there is no guarantee that you will get the letters you want. So why not handcraft your own and decorate them with ornamental sculptural paper motifs? Use the letters to spell a name or if this is too long just their initials, or even to broadcast a message such as 'LUV U'!

To vary the look, the letters would look stunning cut from thick, plain white watercolour paper for a wedding gift. Children will love them too when made from brightly coloured card and decorated with spots and stripes (see page 71). You could glue them flat to thick card to make a funky name panel for a bedroom door.

The letters you choose to make will to some extent determine how you apply the paper-sculptured embellishments. For example, some letters with a dominant upright may be better decorated mainly with diamonds, whereas a more curved form lends itself to a mixture of flowers and diamonds.

Decorated Letters

An enlarged bold, fairground-style font was chosen here, but if you want something simpler, choose a computer font, enlarge it and print it out to use as a template. The three letters shown on the previous page are just a representative sample of how you can decorate letters with the paper-sculptured motifs, but have fun adapting these ideas to your own chosen examples, depending on their style and shape.

You will need:

- 2 x A4 (US Letter) sheets of burgundy lightweight card (per letter)

- scraps of gold lightweight card

- gold and bronze acrylic paint

- wide paintbrush

- basic tool kit (see pages 94–95)

1 **To create the letters** make a template of the letter of your choice (see above) and cut the letter twice from burgundy lightweight card. Use a craft knife to cut around curves for a really smooth finish.

2 Use a dry wide paintbrush to apply a broken layer of gold paint to the fronts of both letters. Leave to dry thoroughly.

3 Brush a thin, broken layer of bronze paint over the gold paint to give a distressed surface finish. Leave the paint to dry thoroughly.

TIP: It is vital to use a completely dry brush to apply the metallic paints and allow the first colour to dry before you add the second to prevent smudging and to achieve a good contrast.

4 To make the spacers between the letters, cut 6cm (2⅜in) wide strips of burgundy card, one for each upright section of the letter, making them slightly shorter than the sections of the letter so that they won't show when they are glued in place. Score and crease a 1cm (⅜in) border down each side of the strips.

5 Place the bottom letter, right way round, on a flat surface. Attach the spacers to the letter. Apply strips of double-sided tape to the tops of the spacers, then position the top letter over them and stick down, aligning the edges of the letters as closely as possible.

TIP: When you stick the two letters together with the spacers, place the letters upright to ensure that when they are joined together they stand upright.

6 To make the decorative motifs cut as many diamond shapes as you require from the burgundy card using the template on page 116. Score on the front and crease where marked.

7 Snip the sides of the diamonds almost to the centre, as marked, then overlap them and glue together.

8 Using a single-hole punch, punch a dot for each diamond from gold lightweight card. Glue a gold dot to the centre of each diamond.

9 Attach the diamonds to the letter with small adhesive foam pads.

10 Punch extra gold dots and glue around the curves of the letter.

11 Cut as many flowers as you require from the burgundy card using the template on page 116. Snip to the centre as marked, then overlap so that the petals bend inwards and glue together. Punch a gold dot for each flower and glue to the centre. Attach to the letter with small adhesive foam pads.

Novelty Name

Spell out a young person's name in style with these dazzling characters. Print out the name twice in your chosen typeface and enlarge on a photocopier to the size that you want. Use as a template to cut out each letter twice from lightweight card. Make spacers for each letter, as in Step 4, page 69. Cut strips of coloured paper and glue to the fronts of two of the letters in horizontal or diagonal stripes, trimming to fit. Punch or cut out small coloured spots and glue to the remaining letter. Glue the spacers between the pairs of letters to finish.

Wedding Wonders

It's much more fun making your own wedding favours than buying them, so here's a great idea for using pretty giftwrap and paper ribbons to make cones that you can match to the wedding colour scheme. The centre of the cone is cut into a V-shape, which forms a heart when the sides are rolled together. An optional refinement is to make a wire stand to present the cone upright – see page 103 for instructions on how to make the stand.

The cones can be used in a variety of creative ways. Place one on each guest's plate with cutlery inside and attach a printed name, or make miniature cones with a tiny pearl button on the front with the guest's name on a paper strip inside. Made in deep red and adorned with a golden arrow, a single cone sends a resounding message on Valentine's Day (see page 77).

These heart-shaped cones, trimmed with a lace-like paper bow and flower button, look wonderfully sophisticated but are in fact very easy to make — a real boon when the pressure of the big occasion is on. Fill them with prettily coloured candy or personalized sweets specially wrapped with a portrait of the happy couple (see page 76).

You will need:

- A4 (US Letter) sheets of pink and white paper

- flower-shaped button

- black and white photocopies of your chosen photo

- wrapped sweets

- basic tool kit (see pages 94–95)

Party Favour Cones

Two different designs of wedding giftwrap have been used to make these cones, but any paper that matches or complements your table setting will be suitable. Giftwrap is ideal because it is thin enough to roll easily yet sturdy enough to hold a handful of sweets. Handmade papers containing flower petals or covered in decorative stitching would also look lovely. Plain Japanese and printed Indian papers are delightful, and again are very strong whilst easy to roll.

1 **To make the cone** cut two 20cm (8in) squares of paper, one pink and one white. Glue the squares together, with wrong sides facing.

2 Cut the heart-shaped lobes from the top corner of the square using the template on page 116.

3 Attach a strip of double-sided tape to the right-hand side of the front of the square on the side of the paper that you want inside the cone. Peel off the backing paper.

4 With the corner of the square facing away from you, roll the sides of the paper around to make a cone shape, overlapping the now left-hand edge with the tape over the right-hand edge. Press the edges together to keep them in place.

5 **To make the ribbon** cut a 1 x 20cm (⅜ x 8in) strip of the leftover pink paper with scallop-edged scissors.

6 Use an eyelet punch with a small head attachment and tack hammer (see page 95) to make holes down the centre of the scallop-edged strip.

7 Loop the ends of the ribbon over to form a bow and secure in place with a piece of double-sided tape. Trim the ends.

8 Stick a square of double-sided tape to the front of the cone, at the centre of the heart. Attach the bow. Glue a button on top.

9 **To make the sweets** cut the photocopied images slightly narrower than the width of the sweets. Apply a strip of double-sided tape to the back of each photo.

TIP: If you don't have a suitable photo, print out the names of the couple and wrap these around the sweets instead.

10 Peel off the backing paper from the tape, then wrap the photos around the sweets, overlapping the paper on the back.

TIP: If using small sweets such as sugared almonds, put them in a clear bag then stick the photo to a tag and tie around the bag top.

Loving Cup

Make a dramatic statement for Valentine's Day with this sumptuous red cone, presented in a wire stand (see page 103) and filled with luxurious chocolates. The cone is constructed just as for the Party Favour Cone but without the bow. For the arrow, paint a wooden kebab stick with gold paint and leave to dry. Cut an arrow tip and flight from gold paper using the templates on page 116, and score and crease where marked. Glue to the stick, then glue the arrow to the front of the cone.

Tea Time

A perfect, everlasting cup of tea – a gift that's guaranteed to go down well on Mother's Day! Looking just like vintage bone china, the rich blue teacup is festooned with rosebuds formed from tightly curled origami paper, with matching saucer opulently edged with gold, and a loving message ingeniously incorporated into the teabag.

The teacup and saucer would look wonderfully elegant in white decorated with pink and gold punched hearts to celebrate a wedding or anniversary. But for a very different effect using the same basic construction techniques, a boldly patterned espresso set would hit the spot for Father's Day (see page 83). Alternatively, the coffee cup alone could be made from lilac paper and decorated with pale yellow punched paper ducks for a cute christening mug.

Make this smart, stylish espresso cup with matching saucer in the same way as the tea set (see page 83) for Father's Day, to let a dad know just how cool he is. And why not package it in an equally tasteful way, nestled in its own presentation box, with an accompanying personalized tag?

You will need:

- A3 (12 x 16½in) sheet of blue medium-weight paper

- A4 (US Letter) sheet of pink spotted lightweight paper

- A4 (US Letter) sheet of gold lightweight paper

- A4 (US Letter) sheets of plain pale pink and dark pink lightweight paper

- scrap of white lightweight paper

- pale pink, dark pink and green origami paper (or lightweight paper)

- A4 (US Letter) sheet of gold lightweight card

- scrap of white lightweight card

- pink narrow ribbon

- heart punch

- basic tool kit (see pages 94–95)

Teacup and Saucer

The cup is formed by curving a section of a circle around until the edges meet to form a cone (see page 99). Using less of the circle will result in a tall, thin cup; more will make a wider, bowl shape. By rolling and curving the paper before assembling the cup and saucer, it is made much more pliable and keeps its shape better when taped. Medium-weight paper is used here, but lightweight card would give a more substantial feel.

1 To make the cup, cut the cup and cup foot from blue medium-weight paper using the templates on page 117. On the back of the cup, score and crease around the inner circle where marked. Snip tabs around the inner edge, as marked.

2 Cut the scallop-edged cup rim from pink spotted paper using the template on page 117. Place the cup face down. Glue the paper around the rim of the cup, aligning the edges exactly.

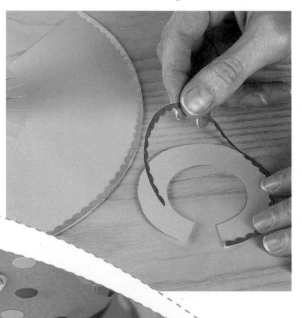

3 Place the cup and cup foot on gold lightweight paper. Draw around the rim of the cup and the outer edge of the cup foot. Cut out using scallop-edged scissors to make narrow borders and glue in place.

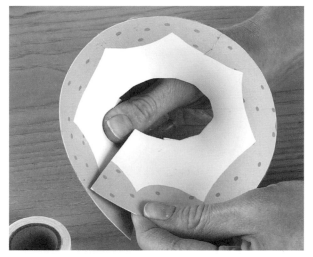

4 Curve the cup around and overlap the sides. Keep in place with double-sided tape. Curve the cup foot around and stick the edges with double-sided tape.

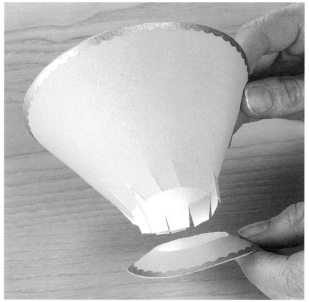

5 Push the tabbed edge of the cup downwards and insert into the top of the cup foot. Press the tabs outwards and glue around the inside edge of the cup foot. Cut a narrow strip of gold paper and glue just above the join.

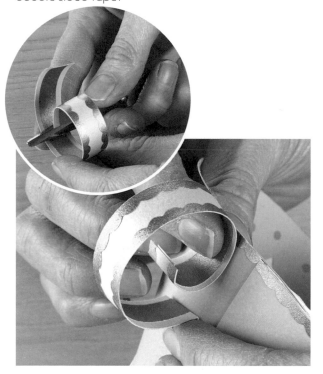

6 Cut the cup handle from blue paper using the template on page 117. Cut two narrow strips of gold paper using scallop-edged scissors to cut one long edge of each and stick to the front of the handle. Cut out and stick a wider gold strip to the back of the handle. Curl the handle by pulling it over the closed blades of a pair of scissors (see page 99). Score and crease the handle on the back where marked. Attach it to the side of the cup with double-sided tape, covering the join.

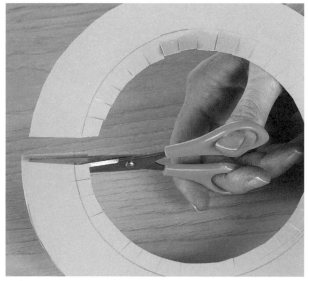

7 **To make the saucer,** cut a saucer from blue paper using the template on page 117. Score around the inner edge on the front where marked and crease. Snip tabs around the inner edge of the saucer, as marked.

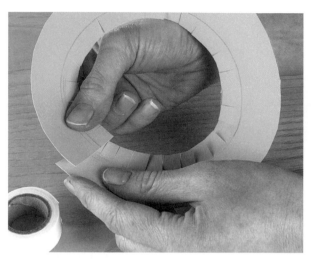

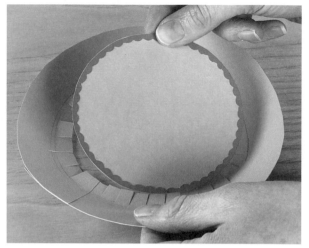

8   Overlap the ends of the saucer and secure with double-sided tape. Press the tabs towards the centre of the saucer. Cut a narrow rim from gold paper to fit around the edge of the saucer.

9   Cut two saucer centres from plain pale pink and one from dark pink lightweight paper using the template on page 117. Trim around the dark pink circle with scallop-edged scissors to make a narrow rim. Glue the dark pink rim to one pink circle, then glue to the saucer front. Glue the other pink circle to the saucer back, covering the tabs.

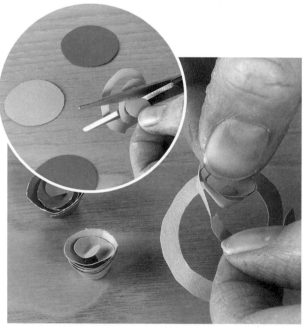

10   Glue the narrow gold rim around the edge of the saucer. Use a single-hole punch to punch dots from gold and white paper. Glue the white dots around the blue rim of the saucer and the gold dots to the pink centre. Glue white and gold dots to the outside and inside of the cup.

11   **To make the rosebuds** cut five buds from pale pink and dark pink origami paper using the template on page 117, cutting around the outside edge. Cut along the spiral cut line from the rim to the centre, as marked. Coil the paper around between your finger and thumb to make rosebud shapes. Secure in place with a dot of glue.

12 Cut 15 leaves from green origami paper using the template on page 117. Score and crease down the centre on the back where marked. Cut 15 narrow strips of gold paper. Glue one along the centre of each leaf. Trim to size. Glue the leaves in clusters of three to the cup. Glue a rosebud at the centre of each group of leaves.

13 **To make the teaspoon** cut a teaspoon from gold lightweight card using the template on page 117. Score and crease, then cut where marked. Overlap the bowl of the spoon to make it three-dimensional and glue. Trim the edges. Gently curve the handle by pulling it over the closed blades of a pair of scissors.

14 **To make the teabag** cut a 6 x 8cm (2 x 3⅛in) rectangle of tracing paper. Fold under 2.5cm (1in) at either side and tape. Fold up the base by 1cm (⅜in) and tape. Punch hearts from pink origami paper and place inside. Fold down the corners diagonally and tape. Attach a length of pink ribbon to the back. Cut a small square of white card and add a dark pink punched heart. Trim the bottom two corners at an angle. Glue a strip of gold paper cut along one edge with scallop-edged scissors to the top. Attach to the other end of the ribbon as a tag.

Coffee Break

The cup shape of this espresso set may differ from that of the teacup, but it is constructed in exactly the same way, using a 6 x 8.5cm (2⅜ x 3¼in) brown paper strip with a scored and tabbed 1cm (⅜in) border along the lower edge glued to a 5.5cm (2¼in) diameter circle. For the saucer, cut a 39cm (15¼in) diameter brown paper circle, then cut a 19cm (7½in) diameter circle from the centre. Curve the paper, overlap the ends and stick with double-sided tape. Cut two 19cm (7½in) diameter brown paper circles for the saucer centre and glue to the front and back. Decorate with strips, spots and diamonds.

Crowning Glory

Transform the children in your life into royalty for a day! These sumptuous-looking items of headgear – a king's crown in gold card and a queen's tiara in pearly lilac card – are simple to cut and score, and they look very effective for parties and special occasions.

To speed up the making process, you can leave out the cut and scored band for the king's crown and add stick-on jewels or rolled-up tissue paper decorations instead. Alternatively, glue a scrap of spotted fun fur around the rim as a fake ermine trim. In the same way, you could ignore the punched holes on the queen's crown and draw on a swirly pattern with a gold metallic pen instead – just remember to add lots of glitter or gems to make up for it!

Elegant scallop-edged fleur-de-lys panels and a decorative band cleverly scored and snipped to create a three-dimensional pattern make this crown fit for a king. Royal red tissue paper completes the picture, which is screwed up before being used to give a slightly textured look, but you can leave it smooth if you prefer.

King's Crown

Lightweight card has been used for both these crowns, as it's stiff enough to keep its shape yet easy to score and crease. Be methodical when you cut and score the decorative band for the crown. Do all the work on one side first, then turn over and complete the job on the back. Don't be tempted to keep turning over as you work, or you will get horribly confused!

You will need:

- A2 (16½ x 23⅜in) sheet of gold lightweight card

- large sheet of red tissue paper

- basic tool kit (see pages 94–95)

1 To make the crown use the template on page 118 to cut the outline from gold lightweight card. Cut out the inner sections of each fleur-de-lys.

> **TIP:** Mark the scoring and cutting lines fairly lightly on the front of the band, but don't be too cautious or you won't be able to see what you are doing. You can always erase the pencil lines afterwards.

2 Score and crease the centres of each of the fleur-de-lys on the front where marked.

3 To make the decorative band cut a 5.5 x 60cm (2¼ x 23½in) band of gold card. Following the template on page 118, mark out the score and cut lines on the front and back of the band, as shown.

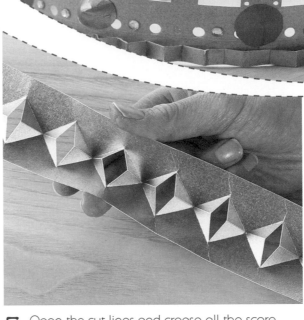

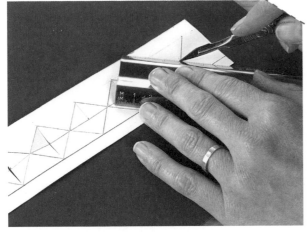

4 Score the lines on the front and back of the band where indicated, then cut where marked on the front.

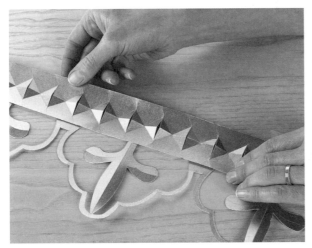

5 Open the cut lines and crease all the score lines you have made on the band so that it becomes three-dimensional.

6 Attach the band to the front of the crown with double-sided tape. Place the crown around the child's head and mark where the ends overlap.

7 **To finish,** roll up pieces of red tissue paper into small balls and glue one to the centre of each fleur-de-lys as jewels. Glue or tape the ends of the crown together.

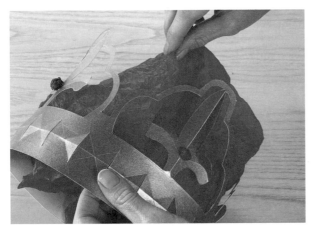

8 Crumple up a sheet of red tissue paper. Open it out, then stick it around the inside rim of the crown in a dome shape so that it fits over the wearer's head.

TIP: Attach a strip of double-sided tape around the inside of the crown band before you stick on the red tissue paper to hold the paper in place immediately; if you press it lightly into position first, you can reposition it if necessary.

Queen's Tiara

A pearlescent lilac card was chosen for this tiara because of its soft, shimmery appearance. The design is very simple to cut, but looks quite sophisticated when it is scored and creased all the way round. The tiara has been decorated here with sequins and punched holes, but all sorts of other decorations would look equally good, especially glitter.

1 **To make the tiara** use the template on page 118 to cut the outline from pearlescent lilac lightweight card.

2 On the front of the tiara, score and crease around the curves where marked.

TIP: Score a faint line along the centre of the crown band to make a guideline to punch along.

3 Place the crown right-side up. Use an eyelet punch fitted with a small head attachment and a tack hammer (see page 95) to make holes around the central section of the tiara.

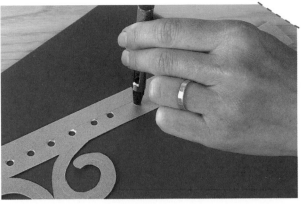

4 Use an eyelet punch fitted with a medium head attachment and a tack hammer to make holes along the centre of the tiara band.

6 Draw around a large coin five times on to gold and purple card. Cut out the circles. Snip each one once from the edge to the centre, then overlap and glue the sides to make domes (see page 99). Glue along the crown band.

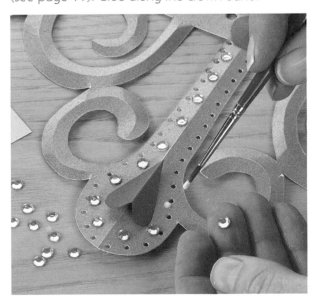

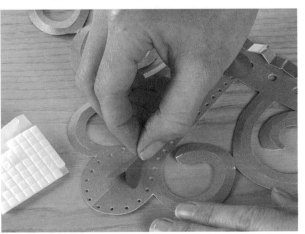

5 **For the crown decorations** cut a long, 5mm (¼in) wide strip of gold card. Concertina-fold the strip (see page 100) and glue it along the lower edge of the tiara band.

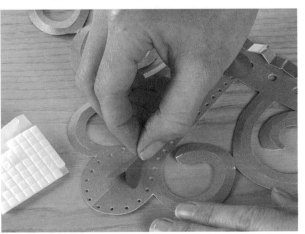

7 Cut a heart from purple card using the template on page 110. Score and crease as marked. Attach to the top of the crown with an adhesive foam pad.

TIP: **If you don't have any gem stones, use holographic adhesive dots or punched silver dots instead.**

8 Glue small gem stones around the central panel of the tiara. Place the tiara around the child's head and mark where the ends overlap. Glue or tape the ends of the tiara together.

Everlasting Flowers

A bouquet of flowers makes a lovely gift for a special birthday or Mother's Day, but sadly never lasts more than a few days. For an everlasting display, make a bunch of beautiful blooms from plain and patterned papers – swirly roses, curly chrysanthemums and spiky petalled marguerites – in blues, pinks and neutrals.

Try to find unusual papers for the flowers, such as the lovely Indian papers with delicate patterns and a sprinkling of white glitter featured here. Black and white newsprint, scrapbooking papers, wallpapers and doll's house papers would also make lovely blooms, as well as vellums and tracing paper, also used here as they are so easy to fold and curl. Metallics would be perfect for Christmas, or for a silver or golden wedding anniversary gift.

The flowers would look lovely arranged in a coordinating vase. Alternatively, create a fabulous bouquet by begging some custom-made wrapping from your local florist's shop, which will usually have a selection of very pretty papers and sheets of printed acetate. Add a sumptuous paper ribbon or paper lace tie for a finishing flourish.

Flower Sprays

When attaching the tissue paper to the flower stem, turn the wire rather than the paper. This will roll the paper quickly and smoothly around the wire without creasing it. Instead of tracking down and cutting wire to length, you could try using florists' wire. This is very pliable and easy to manipulate, and comes in just the right length to make flower stems.

1 **To make the flower stems** cut a 30cm (12in) length of the wire with pliers. Cut a 3cm (1⅛in) wide strip of green tissue paper. Stick a piece of double-sided tape to one end of the strip and wrap it around the wire. Glue in place at the end of the wire. The tops of the marguerite and rose stems are looped and the chrysanthemum stems are straight. To make the loops, wrap the ends of the stems around a pencil.

2 **To make the rose** cut a 10cm (4in) diameter circle from pink medium-weight paper. Lightly draw a spiral on to the circle and cut around it. Trim the end of the spiral into a rounded shape. Curl the paper over the closed blades of a pair of scissors (see page 99).

3 Roll the paper around to make a rose shape. Overlap the ends and keep them in place with double-sided tape. Take a looped stem, and use pliers to bend over the loop at right angles. Attach the rose to the top of the loop with PVA (white) glue. Glue a short strip of green tissue paper around the loop to hide it. Cut two rose leaves from green medium-weight paper using the template on page 114. Glue below the rose.

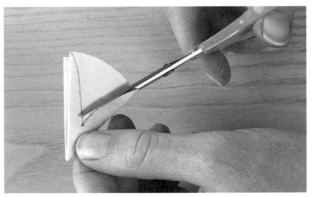

4 To make the chrysanthemum, fold a 15 x 30cm (6 x 12in) rectangle of tracing or patterned paper in half. Score a 1cm (⅜in) border below the folded edge, then snip all the way along the paper, as far as the fold. Stick double-sided tape along the border, then roll around a straight stem and press firmly in place.

5 Working around the flower head a layer at a time, pull each narrow strip over the closed blades of a pair of scissors to curl it. Cut two chrysanthemum leaves from green paper using the template on page 114 and tape them to the stem, below the flower head. Curl the leaves, then cover the bases with a short strip of green tissue paper.

6 To make the marguerite cut a 10cm (4in) circle from patterned paper. Fold it in half, then into quarters. Draw a half petal adjoining each of the two folded sides, as shown. Carefully snip around the pencil lines, taking care not to cut through the folded edges.

7 Open out the flower, then tape a looped stem to the reverse. Draw around a small coin on to contrasting paper. Cut out and glue to the flower centre. Cut two marguerite leaves from green paper using the template on page 114 and glue to the stem, below the flower. Cover the bases of the leaves with a short strip of green tissue paper.

8 To present the flowers as a bouquet make as many flowers as you require, then place them on a sheet of paper. Wrap the paper around the flowers, then tie with a length of paper ribbon.

Basic Tool Kit

The following is a guide to choosing and using the essential items that you will need for any paper-sculpting project. Before you begin, make sure you have assembled this basic tool kit together and keep it to hand and in good order.

Tracing Paper and Pencil

These can be used to transfer templates printed at full size to paper and card (see pages 104–119). Trace the template first using a pencil, then scribble over the lines on the back of the tracing paper with the pencil, flip the tracing over again and re-draw over the lines to transfer the design or shape. Use an HB pencil for tracing to achieve a precise line without smudging.

Scissors

Choose small, general papercraft or dressmaking scissors with slim, sharp blades and pointed ends, since they are comfortable to handle and will cut small, fiddly shapes with ease. Buy the best-quality scissors you can, as they will stay sharp and cut with precision for longer.

Craft Knife

For general everyday cutting, a scalpel with detachable blades is a good choice. The handles are lightweight, very comfortable to hold and so easy to manipulate that you can cut with great precision and accuracy. The handles and blades come in different sizes – a number 3 handle with a number 10 blade is suitable for most paper-sculpting purposes. The blades come in packs of five and are inexpensive, so change the blade regularly, as they do get blunt relatively quickly. When not in use, insert the sharp blade into a cork to prevent accidents.

Cutting Mat

This is absolutely essential to use when cutting with a craft knife. It has a rubberized surface that seals itself after each cut, so you always have a perfectly smooth surface to work on. The surface of the mat also grips the blade of the craft knife slightly and prevents it from sliding across the work surface. Cutting mats come in a variety of sizes, but a larger one will obviously give you enough scope to cut long pieces of paper.

Metal Ruler

These are much more accurate and precise than plastic ones for measuring and marking out, which tend to get chipped after a while. One 60cm (23½in) long is useful for large pieces of paper.

Metal Safety Ruler

Always use a metal safety ruler with a craft knife. It has a channel running down the middle to keep fingers safely away from sharp blades. Don't be tempted to cut against a plastic or ordinary metal ruler, as you will take chunks out of the side of it and are in danger of cutting your fingers too.

Decorative-edged scissors

Small, pointed scissors

Craft knife and cutting mat

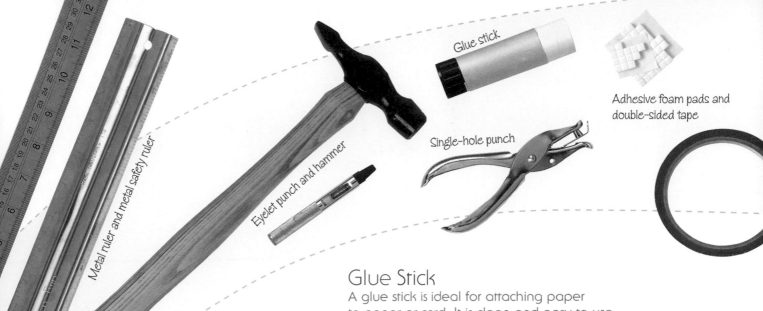

Glue stick

Adhesive foam pads and
double-sided tape

Single-hole punch

Eyelet punch and hammer

Metal ruler and metal safety ruler

Pair of Compasses

These are used to draw circles of
precise dimensions. The best kind
have an adjustable metal bar running
between the two halves to keep
them rigid while you work. They are also
available with built-in, replaceable pencil
leads to save you attaching a pencil.

Decorative-Edged Scissors

Scissors with decoratively shaped blades are
fun to use and come in lots of great designs,
including zigzag, scallop and large scallop
featured in the projects in this book. These
scissors are available with plastic or metal blades, but
metal-bladed ones tend to cut more cleanly.

Eyelet Punch and Hammer

This kind of punch is perfect for piercing
very small holes, which are great for adding
decorative detail to your projects. Eyelet punches
come with detachable heads in a variety
of sizes. You can buy hammers specifically
designed to use with eyelet punches, but
they are quite expensive, so use an ordinary
115g (4oz) tack hammer instead.

Single-Hole Punch

This makes a slightly larger hole than a stationery
hole punch that punches a double set of holes.
Single-hole punches make precision punching
very easy, as you can mark exactly where the
hole should go and then punch directly on top
of the mark.

Glue Stick

A glue stick is ideal for attaching paper
to paper or card. It is clean and easy to use,
has a strong adhesion once dry and can be
applied accurately. It is also repositionable for
a couple of minutes after applying.

PVA (White) Glue

This is the adhesive to use for sticking 3D shapes
to a surface when a glue stick and double-sided
tape are not appropriate. It will keep thick card
motifs in place or folded shapes that have only
a very small surface area where you can apply
glue and therefore need a strong bond. Opt for
the high-tack version, which is very sticky and
fast drying, so it doesn't hold up the making
process. It is also great for attaching small items
such as gem stones and sequins to your work.
For papier mâché (see page 20), use traditional
PVA (white) glue diluted in a ratio of 60/40 with
water, which dries very hard and gives a smooth
surface on which to paint.

Double-Sided Tape

Use this tape for keeping heavyweight paper
firmly in place. It is also great for holding paper
that has been manipulated in some way, for
example when rolled, as normal paper or PVA
(white) glue wouldn't dry quickly enough to
keep it in place. It comes in several widths,
1cm (⅜in) wide being the most useful, although
wider tape is more suitable if the paper is
particularly heavy.

Adhesive Foam Pads

These small foam squares with adhesive on
either side are perfect for attaching 3D shapes
to flat surfaces, and have a very strong bond.
Their compact size means that they can be
placed inconspicuously and hidden from view.
You can cut them to a specific size or shape
if you need to. They also have the effect of
raising elements from the surface, giving the
design a dimensional feel.

Papers and Card

These all-important materials for paper sculpting come in a huge range – plain and printed, opaque and translucent, and in a multitude of different colours. Making the appropriate choice for the purpose you have in mind is key to achieving the best results, and thickness is a vital consideration.

Paper Weights

Paper comes in a variety of thicknesses, known as 'weights', ranging from thin (lightweight) to thick (heavyweight). Weights are measured in grams per square metre (gsm).

Type of paper	Weight in gsm
Lightweight	80–120
Medium-weight	120–150
Heavyweight	150–250

Plain papers

Lightweight paper, such as writing or photocopier paper, is quite flimsy, so won't stand rough handling. However, it is very flexible and will hold its shape well if you manipulate it in some way, for example by curling it (see page 99). If you find a piece of lightweight paper that you really love, simply mount it on to a sheet of white medium-weight paper before you use it to give it added strength.

Medium-weight paper is highly versatile, being strong yet easy to cut, score, fold, stitch and do virtually anything else you want to do with it! The plain artists' papers called mi-teintes or demi-teintes are particularly appealing, as they come in a huge variety of interesting and subtle shades.

Heavyweight paper is useful for larger projects where you want an item to keep its shape without warping or buckling. It is more difficult to cut and score, and usually needs strong glue such as PVA (white) glue (see page 95) to stick it.

Card and Foam Board

Card is also measured in gsm, starting at 150gsm, which is classified as thin card. You will find card used in many of the projects, mainly to add strength to the designs, that is around 170–180gsm. This weight of card has good flexibility and folds cleanly, especially when scored.

Card of around 210–240gsm in weight is sturdy and keeps its shape very well, so is ideal for boxes and general modelling. Card heavier than this is very tough to cut. A more practical alternative is to use 5–7mm (³⁄₁₆–¹⁄₄in) thick foam board. Employed extensively for display and exhibition work, foam board comes in sheets in a variety of sizes. It has a lightweight polystyrene core sandwiched between two sheets of very thin card and is extremely easy to cut with a craft knife.

Tissue paper

Tissue Paper

This comes in a variety of fantastic colours. Although very thin and fragile, it is worth persevering with because it is so easy to manipulate in a number of creative ways – it can be crumpled, rolled, curled and folded with ease, and makes lovely flower heads (see pages 90–93). It is also ideal for adding depth and volume to a shape, as you can use many layers without adding much weight.

Tracing Paper and Vellum

Tracing paper is a joy to use. It is translucent with an ethereal quality, very strong, exceptionally easy to cut and fold, wonderful to curl and keeps its shape very well. It comes in sheets and books of plain white paper, and different colours, when it is generally known as vellum.

Printed Papers

There are so many wonderful examples available that you will be spoilt for choice. For many paper-sculpting projects, subtle patterns such as tiny polka dots and small-scale paisleys are preferable to large patterns, which can distract the eye from the overall form of the item. Keep on the lookout for unusual (and often free) sources of printed paper. Wallpaper sample books, for example, are great to use, as are illustrated food labels, adverts in foreign magazines and newspapers (especially those with coloured pages) and photocopies of children's drawings and handwriting.

Handmade Papers

All of the above papers are machine-made, but a great variety of handmade papers are also on offer. Handmade papers look lovely, as you can often see the plant fibres used in their production on the surface of the paper. Like machine-made papers and cards, they come in lots of different thicknesses, from very thin and translucent to very thick and card-like. You can use handmade papers in exactly the same way as the machine-made types, but if the one you like is very thin, mount it first on to medium-weight paper to strengthen it.

Vellum

Printed papers

Handmade papers

Essential Techniques

Basic paper-sculpting techniques are very straightforward and easy to master with a little practice. The most important points to remember are to use the right weight of paper (see page 96), measure precisely before you begin and cut or score carefully to achieve the best results.

Scoring

A simple way to add dimension and modelling to a flat piece of paper is to score it. Scoring simply means cutting halfway through the paper before you fold it, enabling paper to be folded precisely and cleanly. This gives the form sharply defined shadows when light falls upon it and makes it three-dimensional. The paper will bend away from the scored line, so scoring can be carried out on either side of the paper.

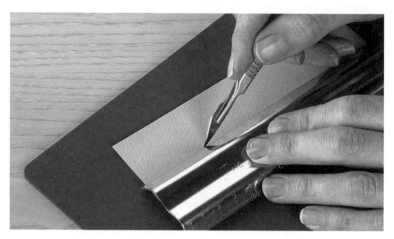

1 Place your paper on a flat surface, with the correct side for scoring facing up. Draw a faint pencil guideline, then place a metal safety ruler against the line. Draw the back of the wrong side of a craft-knife blade along the score line, pressing just hard enough to break the surface of the paper but not to cut right through it. Be sure to keep your fingers away from the craft-knife blade.

2 Take the paper in both hands and squeeze very gently along the score line, widening the split. Once you have opened the scored line to the end, fold along the score and crease firmly.

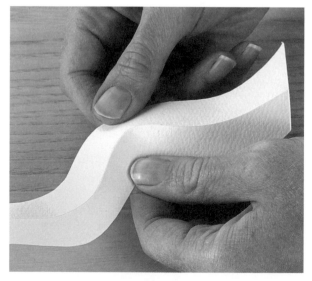

3 To score a curved shape, lightly draw a score line down the centre of the paper, following the curve of the shape. Once the paper is scored, squeeze gently along the line to shape the paper and make it three-dimensional.

Curling

Paper may be curled in several ways, tightly or loosely, depending on its weight and the size of the piece. Paper, like fabric, has a definite grain, and it is much easier to curl it with the grain rather than against it. To find the grain, take a sample of the paper and tear it in half. If it leaves a ragged edge and is difficult to control, you are tearing against the grain. If it tears easily, with a smooth line, you are tearing with the grain.

Curling Light/Medium-Weight Strips

To tightly curl narrow strips of lightweight to medium-weight paper, and lightweight card, hold firmly in one hand and pull the paper over the closed blades of a pair of scissors. Don't pull thin paper too hard, or it will tear.

Curling Heavier Paper and Card

Find the grain of the paper first, then roll it tightly, with the grain, around a pencil. Hold in place for a few seconds to keep the shape.

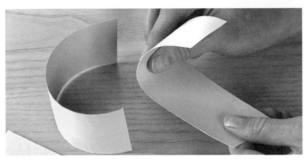

Rolling Paper

To give paper a gently rolled effect, hold it firmly in one hand and pull along the length between finger and thumb several times. It can then be curved into whatever shape you need, and will fold into gentle waves with ease.

Curving

Curving and overlapping the sides of a flat shape will raise its surface and make it three-dimensional. Circles that are treated in this way become cones, one of the most frequently used forms in paper sculpture. They are great for making flower centres (see pages 6–7), jewels (see page 89) and fruits (see page 45). Lightweight to medium-weight paper is best to use; anything heavier is too stiff to keep its shape once curved.

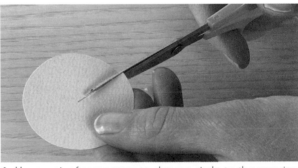

1 Use a pair of compasses to draw a circle to the required size on paper and cut it out. Snip a straight line from the edge to the centre of the circle.

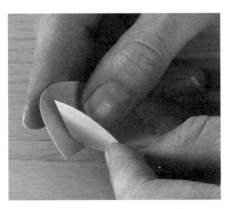

2 Gently curl the paper by pulling it between finger and thumb so that the surface rises slightly.

3 Curve the edges of the circle around on top of each other until the cone is the desired height. Draw a line where the edges overlap. Spread glue on the edges and press together, overlapping where marked.

Pleating

This decorative effect is used principally to add strength and fullness to paper, especially when forming rounded shapes. It is also useful for producing concertina-folded pages for small books and mini albums. It works best with lightweight and medium-weight paper and lightweight card – anything heavier gets unsightly creases when it is pleated. It is also difficult to make evenly spaced folds in heavy paper and card, as you have to allow for the thickness of the paper when you measure.

1 Mark the width of the pleats along the top and bottom edge of both sides of the paper. Remember to alternate the spacing of the lines on the front and back to achieve a concertina effect when the paper is folded.

2 Lay the paper out flat. Place your ruler vertically, joining up each corresponding pair of marks, and score between them (see Step 1, page 98). Turn the paper over and repeat on the other side.

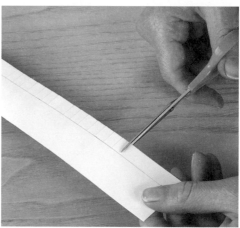

3 Carefully pleat the paper, pinching along the scored lines to open them before each fold is made (see Step 2, page 98).

Tabbed Walls

This is the easiest way to make a complex shape three-dimensional. A paper or card strip is snipped into tabs and scored along one or both sides, which can then be manipulated to follow curves, circles and other shapes and glued to the shape to create a side or glued to join two shapes if tabbed on both sides.

1 Cut the wall to the width and length you require. Draw a 1–1.5cm (⅜–⅝in) deep border along one or both sides of the wall. Snip carefully along the wall as far as the border, approximately every 1.5cm (⅝in).

2 Place the wall right-side up on a cutting mat. Score along the border with the wrong side of a craft-knife blade (see Step 1, page 98). Fold under the tabs.

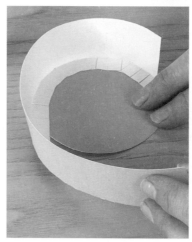

3 To attach the wall to a curved shape, curl it between finger and thumb to make it pliable. Spread glue on the tabs and curve the wall around your shape, matching the wall to the profile of the shape as precisely as possible. Press down the tabs, trim the wall to size and glue and overlap the ends.

Surface Treatment

Flat areas of paper can be given added visual interest by altering the surface in a decorative way. Breaking up the surface creates shadows that emphasize the modelling of the shape. Cutting away or punching out areas is very effective and gives a fun, lively feel to the paper.

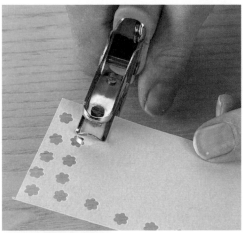

Punching

The simplest way to enliven a flat area of paper is to remove areas with a punch. Use a single-hole punch or a shaped punch, as here. You can punch out a random, all-over pattern or just punch out a selected few small areas.

Cutting Out Triangles

Draw a series of small triangles on paper, then cut along two sides to make 'V' shapes and lift up so that the triangles stand upright. This is a good technique for creating the effect of grass or feathers, and the shapes will throw quite dramatic shadows. A series of semicircles can be made in the same way, using a small coin to draw around, to create fish scales or abstract patterns in large areas of paper.

Stitching

You can use stitching to hold paper together but at the same time create a really interesting visual effect. A sewing machine is shown here, but hand stitching is just as effective. Sewing paper is simple to do and in fact is easier than sewing fabric because there are no frayed edges to deal with.

1 You can't pin two pieces of paper together without marking them, but they will slide around and move if they are not held together in some way. The solution is to use small pieces of masking or magic tape to keep the paper in place while you sew, which can then be gently peeled off afterwards.

2 Use a long straight stitch and a fairly thick needle – one that is designed for use on denim or leather is ideal. Sew carefully and slowly, and when you reach a corner, stop the machine, lift the presser foot and turn the paper before continuing to sew. If you try to turn it while stitching, the paper will probably tear.

3 To finish off a row of stitching, lift the presser foot, remove the paper and cut the threads, leaving long ends. Turn the paper face down and pull the top thread through to the back with a pin.

Making a Keepsake Box

This box with a separate lid is featured on pages 36–41 as a keepsake box card in two different designs, one containing baby bootees to mark the birth of a new baby and the other a wedding cake to celebrate a marriage. Use a medium-weight card, either in a plain colour, as here, or with a printed pattern. You could also cover the box with decorative giftwrap.

1 Cut the box from medium-weight card using the diagram on page 119. Working over a cutting mat, score all round the sides and along the tabs on the back where marked (see Step 1, page 98).

3 Fold in the tabs at the corners of the box and lid. Spread a thin layer of PVA (white) glue on to the tabs or attach strips of double-sided tape. Position the tabs against the box and lid sides, making sure that the edges match exactly. Press the tabs to secure.

2 Cut a lid from the same card using the diagram on page 119. Score on the back, then snip across the corners where marked. Fold up the sides of the box and lid. Crease all the fold lines firmly so that the sides stand upright.

Making a Lidded Box

This baker's style cake box is featured in the Sweet Cupcakes section on page 6 for presenting a single cupcake, but you can also make a larger box to hold several cupcakes. Diagrams for the two sizes of box are given on page 119. They are quick and easy to make, and strong yet lightweight.

1 Cut the box from lightweight card using the diagram on page 119. Place on a cutting mat and carefully score the fold lines where marked (see Step 1, page 98).

3 Spread a thin layer of PVA (white) glue on to the tabs or attach strips of double-sided tape. Position the tabs against the box sides, making sure that the edges match exactly. Press the tabs to secure.

2 Fold up the sides where marked and fold the tabs inwards. Crease all the fold lines firmly so that the sides stand upright.

Making a Wire Stand

The party favour and Valentine cones featured on pages 72–77 look fabulous presented in wire stands so that they can sit upright. You will need two cylindrical objects to form loops in the wire: one about 25cm (10in) in diameter, such as a large food can, and the other 20cm (8in) in diameter, such as a spray can.

1 Cut a 40cm (16in) length of wire. Wrap one end around the larger cylinder and use pliers to twist the free end of the wire around to secure it.

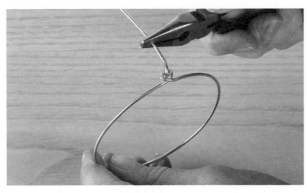

2 Slide the wire loop off the cylinder. To make a stem, bend the remaining wire down at right angles.

3 Measure 20cm (8in) down the stem and use pliers to bend the wire up at right angles.

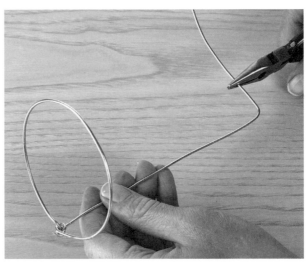

4 Using pliers, turn the wire out at a 45° angle to make it easier to form into a loop.

5 Place the wire around the smaller cylinder and overlap the ends, twisting them tightly together to make a loop.

6 Slide the wire loop off the cylinder. Snip off the excess wire, then twist in and turn under the free end of the wire.

Templates

Many of the following templates are printed at full size, ready to use. If no enlargement is given, use actual size. Those templates that are reduced in size will need to be enlarged on a photocopier at the percentage specified.

Using Templates

Many of the projects in this book have templates for you to trace (see page 94) or photocopy and transfer to the paper of your choice, presented on the pages that follow. If the paper needs to be scored, this will be indicated on the template by a solid or a broken coloured line. The scoring for front and back are colour coded, so carefully study the key above and follow the coloured guidelines when using the templates.

1 A green solid score line indicates that the scoring is to be done on the front of the paper. Transfer the outline of the template and the solid lines to the paper and cut out the shape. Score along the solid lines (see Step 1, page 98).

2 A blue broken score line indicates that the scoring is to be done on the back of the paper. Turn the shape over, then transfer the broken lines to the paper and score them in the same way.

3 When you have completed the scoring, press along the edges on the front and back to crease the paper and make it three-dimensional (see Step 2, page 98).

Sweet Cupcakes (pages 6–11)

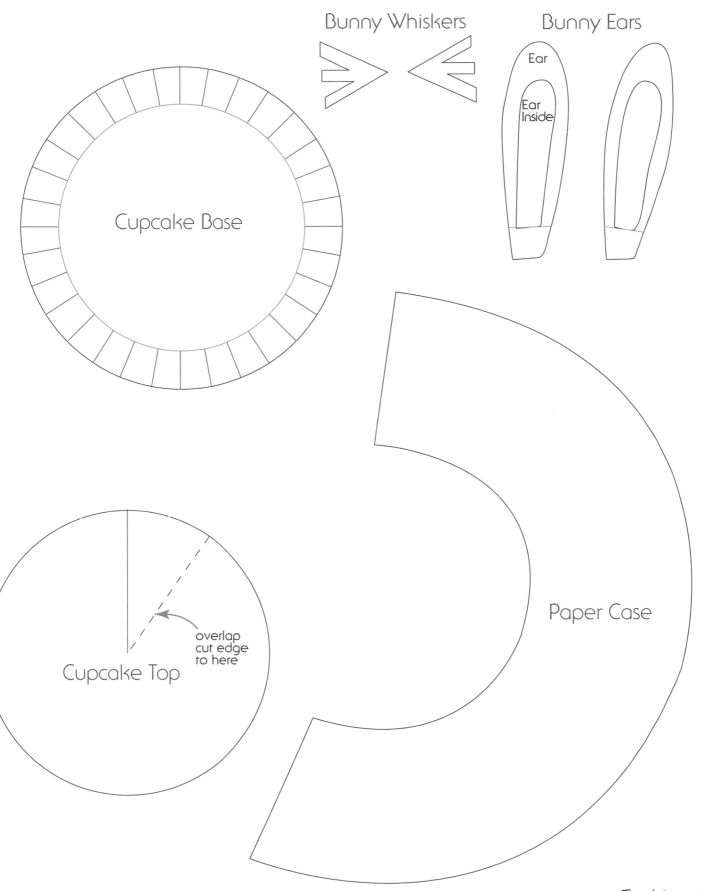

Cupcake Base

Bunny Whiskers

Bunny Ears

Ear

Ear Inside

Paper Case

Cupcake Top

overlap cut edge to here

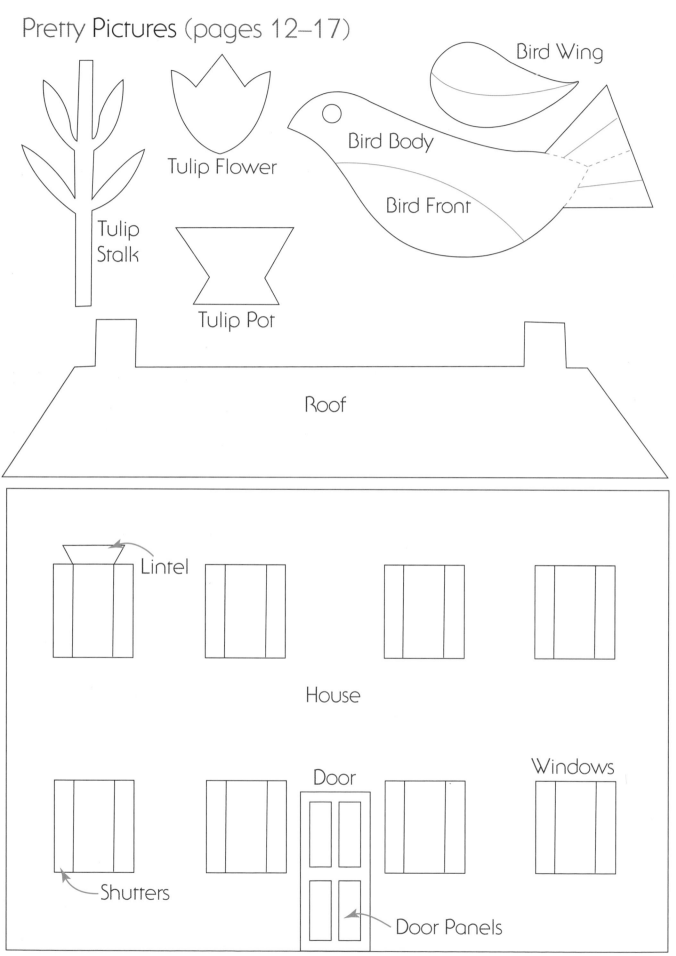

Bird Wing

Bird Body

Bird Front

Tulip Flower

Tulip Stalk

Tulip Pot

Roof

Lintel

House

Windows

Door

Shutters

Door Panels

Pretty Pictures (pages 12–17)

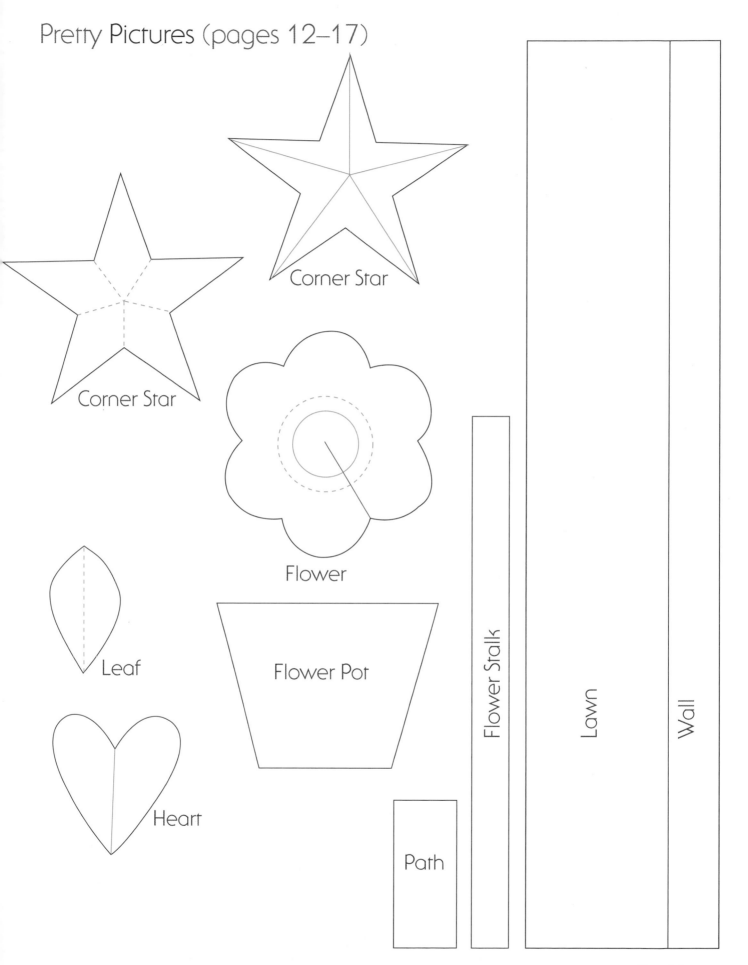

Corner Star

Corner Star

Flower

Leaf

Heart

Flower Pot

Path

Flower Stalk

Lawn

Wall

Fantasy Fairies (pages 18–22)

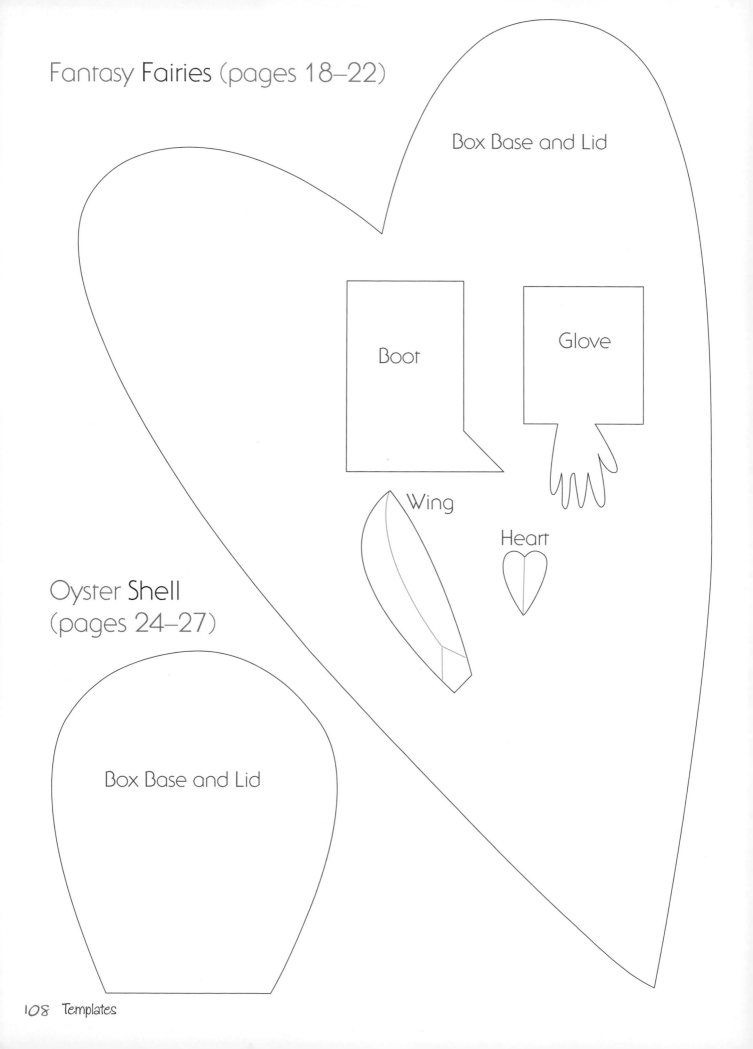

Box Base and Lid

Boot

Glove

Wing

Heart

Oyster Shell
(pages 24–27)

Box Base and Lid

Fabulous Frames (pages 28–33)

(Enlarge by 200%)

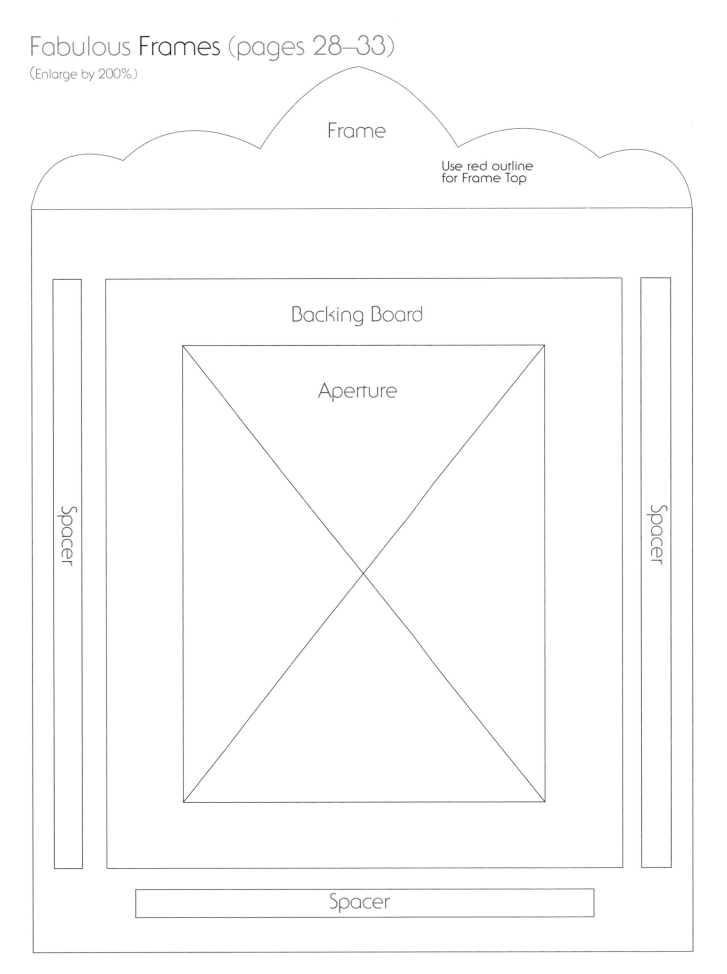

Frame

Use red outline
for Frame Top

Backing Board

Aperture

Spacer

Spacer

Spacer

A Special Anniversary (pages 28–33)

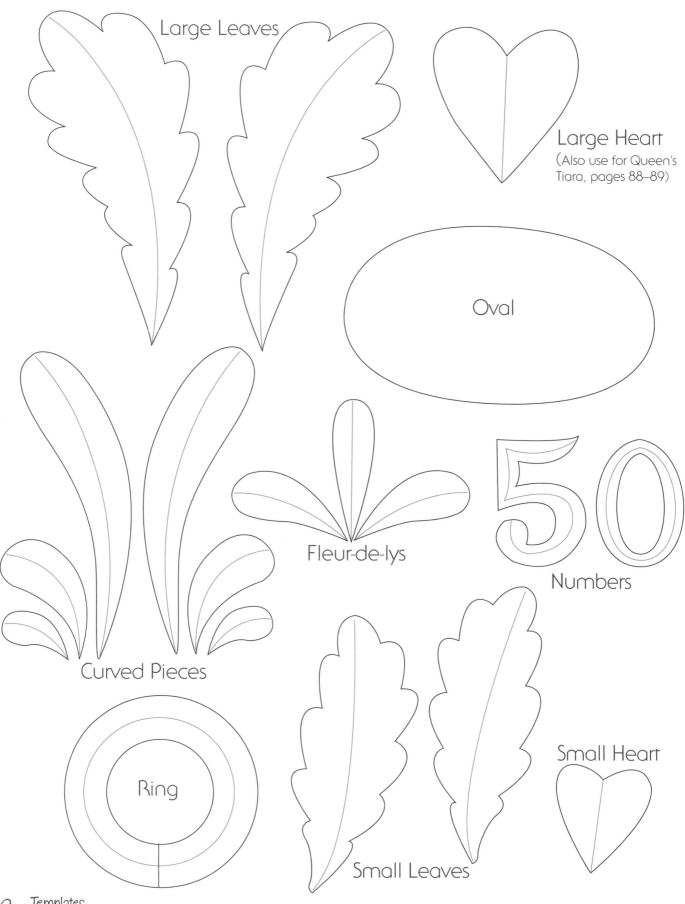

Large Leaves

Large Heart
(Also use for Queen's Tiara, pages 88–89)

Oval

Fleur-de-lys

50
Numbers

Curved Pieces

Ring

Small Leaves

Small Heart

Perfectly Framed (pages 34–35)

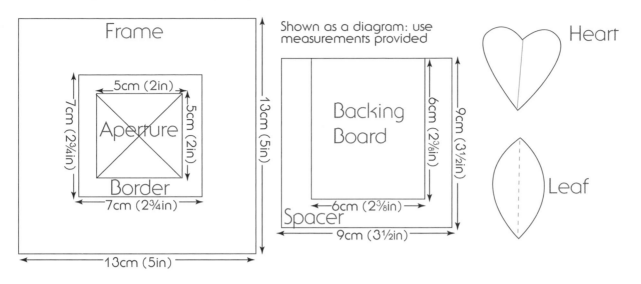

Frame

5cm (2in)

7cm (2¾in)

Aperture

5cm (2in)

Border

7cm (2¾in)

13cm (5in)

13cm (5in)

Shown as a diagram: use measurements provided

Backing Board

6cm (2⅜in)

9cm (3½in)

Spacer

6cm (2⅜in)

9cm (3½in)

Heart

Leaf

Baby Bootees (pages 36–39)

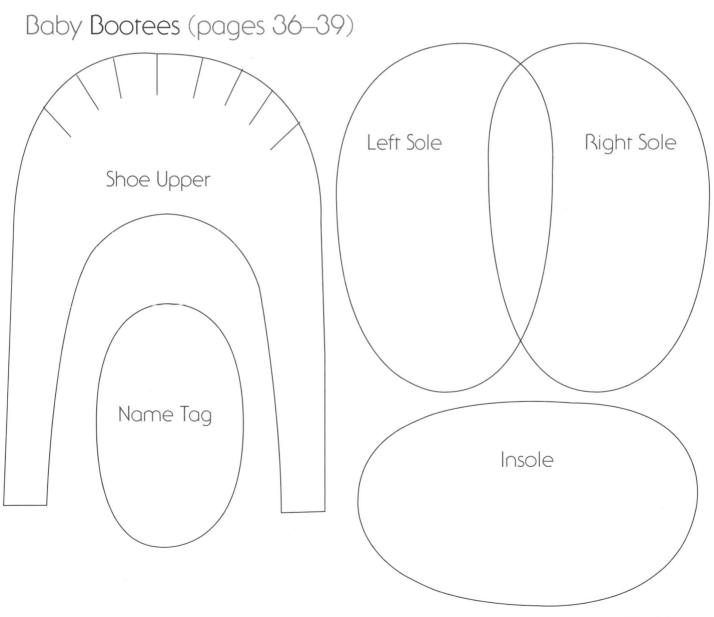

Shoe Upper

Name Tag

Left Sole

Right Sole

Insole

Wedding Day (pages 40–41)

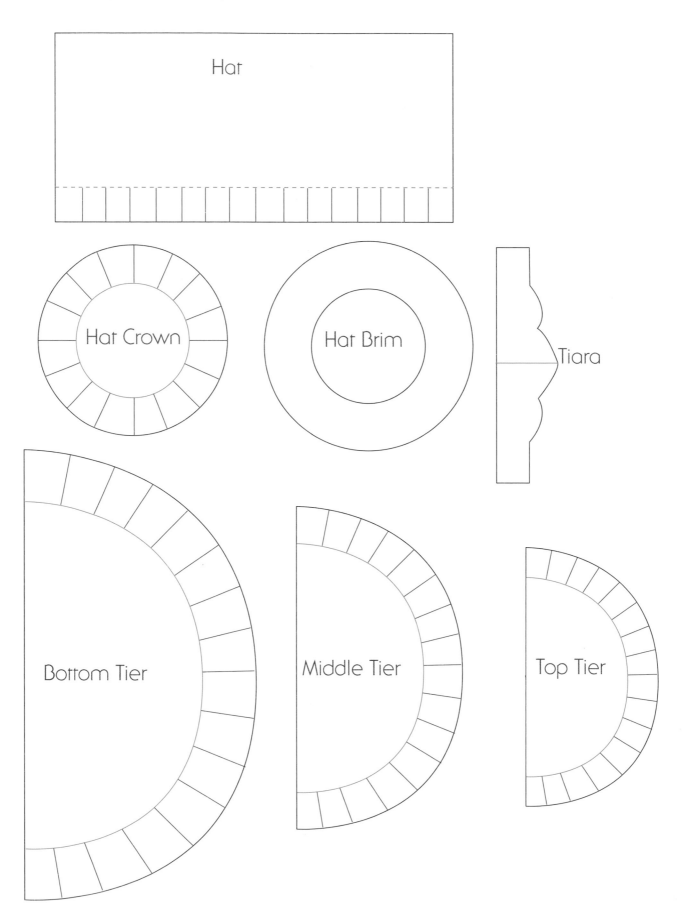

Hat

Hat Crown

Hat Brim

Tiara

Bottom Tier

Middle Tier

Top Tier

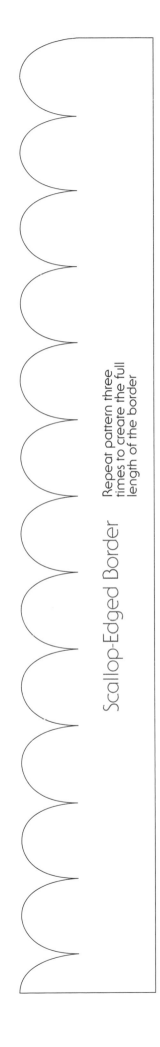

Scallop-Edged Border

Repeat pattern three times to create the full length of the border

Piece of Cake (pages 42–47)

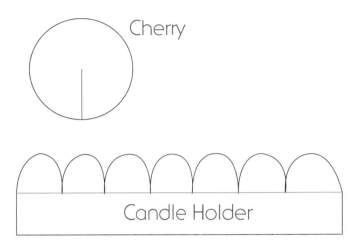

Cherry

Candle Holder

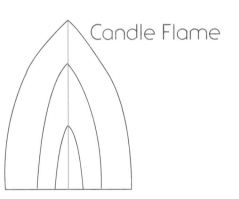

Candle Flame

Gorgeous Garlands
(pages 48–53)

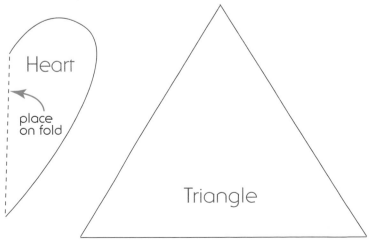

Heart

place on fold

Triangle

Glamorous Gift Bag
(pages 58–61) (Enlarge by 200%)

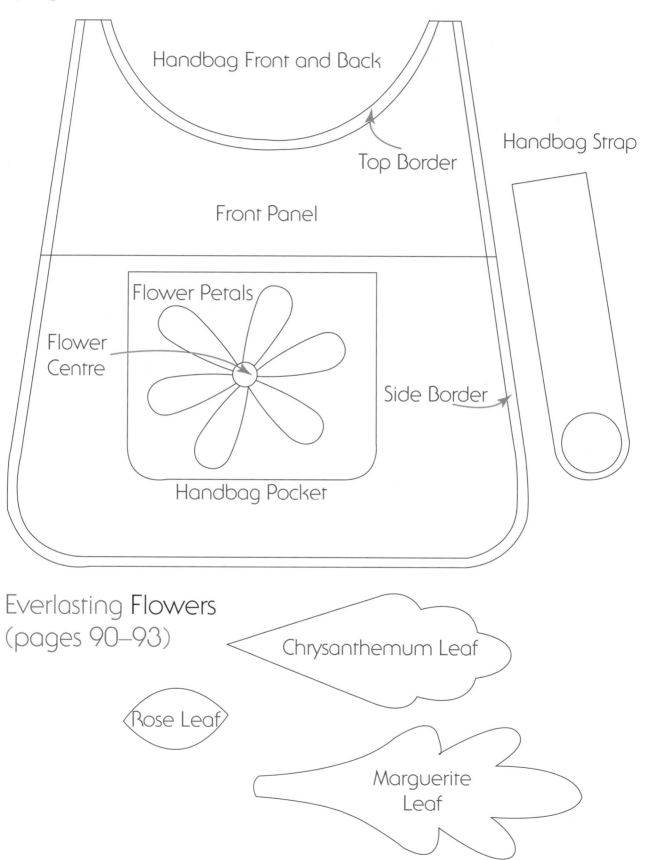

Handbag Front and Back

Top Border

Handbag Strap

Front Panel

Flower Petals

Flower Centre

Side Border

Handbag Pocket

Everlasting Flowers
(pages 90–93)

Chrysanthemum Leaf

Rose Leaf

Marguerite Leaf

Bag It Up (pages 62–65)

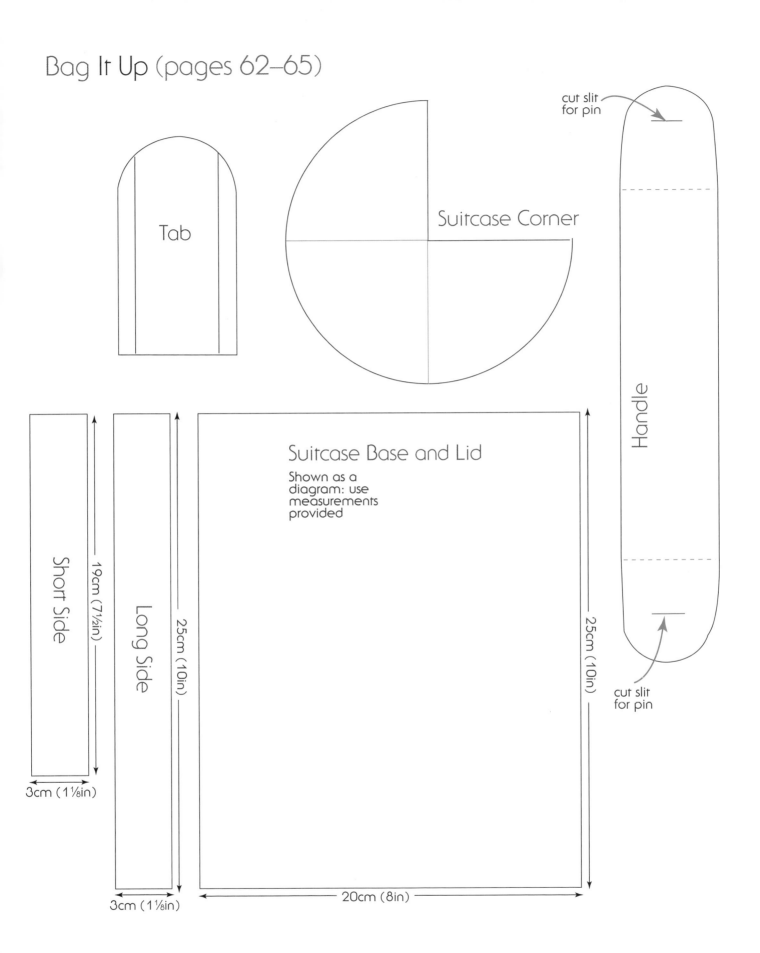

Tab

Suitcase Corner

cut slit
for pin

Handle

Suitcase Base and Lid

Shown as a
diagram: use
measurements
provided

cut slit
for pin

Short Side

19cm (7½in)

Long Side

25cm (10in)

25cm (10in)

3cm (1⅛in)

3cm (1⅛in)

20cm (8in)

Bag It Up (pages 62–65)

Travel Labels

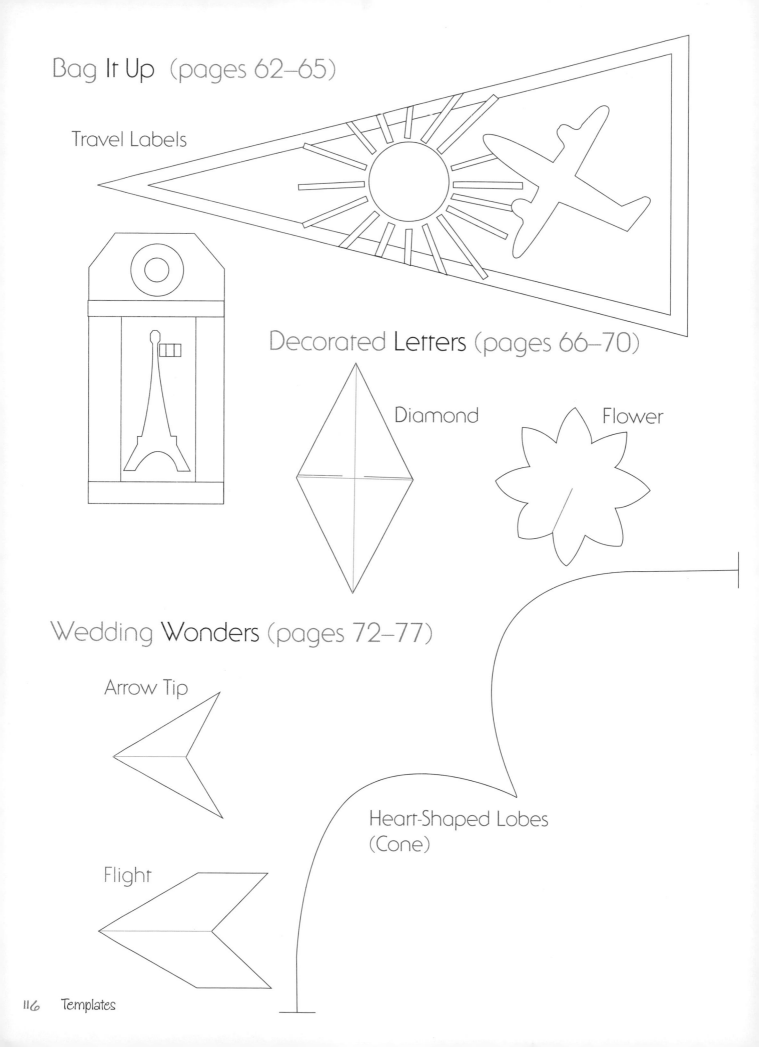

Decorated Letters (pages 66–70)

Diamond

Flower

Wedding Wonders (pages 72–77)

Arrow Tip

Heart-Shaped Lobes
(Cone)

Flight

Tea Time (pages 78–83)
(Enlarge by 200%)

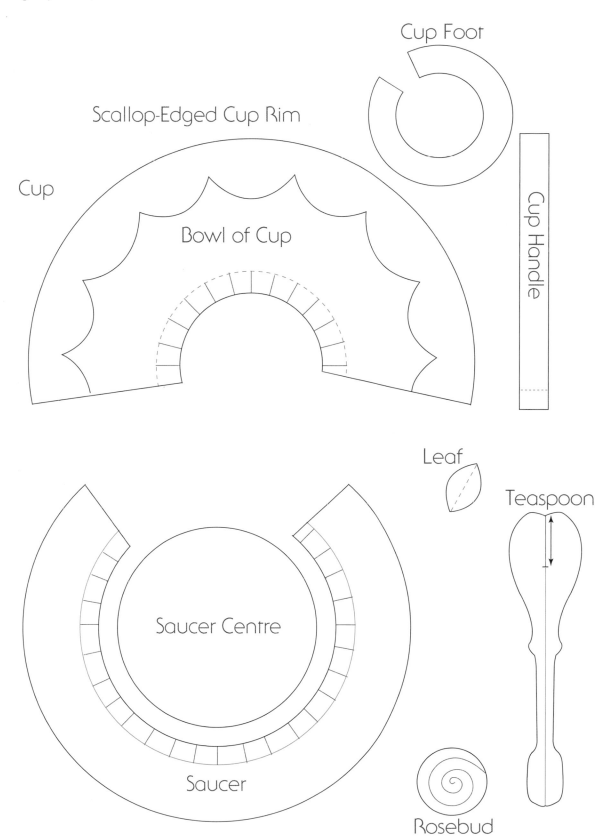

Cup Foot

Scallop-Edged Cup Rim

Cup

Bowl of Cup

Cup Handle

Leaf

Teaspoon

Saucer Centre

Saucer

Rosebud

Crowning Glory (pages 84–89)

(Enlarge by 200%)

King's
Crown

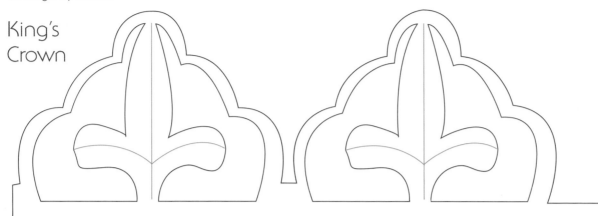

Repeat this section for full length of crown,
adding extra width to the band as required
to fit around the recipient's head

Decorative Band (King's Crown)

Front

Back

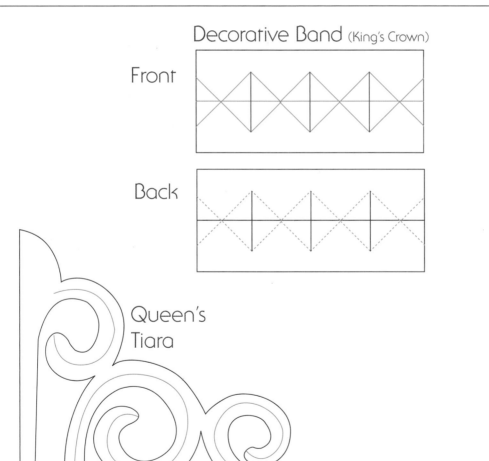

Queen's
Tiara

punch holes along this line

Repeat this section for
full length of tiara

Keepsake Box
(pages 102 and 36–41)

Lidded Boxes
(pages 102 and 6–11)

Shown as diagrams: use measurements provided

Keepsake Box Base

7cm (2¾in)

32cm (12½in)

25cm (5in)

7cm (2¾in)

7cm (2¾in)

24cm (9½in)

Keepsake Box Lid

36cm (14⅛in)

6cm (2⅛in)

6cm (2⅛in)

30cm (6in)

Large Lidded Box

28cm (11in)

10cm (4in)

10cm (4in)

10cm (4in)

80cm (31⅛in)

28cm (11in)

10cm (4in)

28cm (11in)

28cm (11in)

Small Lidded Box

5cm (2in)

32cm

10cm (4in)

10cm (4in)

5cm (2in)

10cm (4in)

5cm (2in)

5cm (2in)

Suppliers

UK Suppliers

Book Ends
66 Exmouth Market
London EC1R 4QP
Tel: 020 7713 8555
Email: info@
bookendslondon.co.uk
*Specialists in paper crafts,
origami paper and many
other craft products*

www.e-crafts.co.uk
Tel: 01384 230000
*Wide range of
decorative papers*

Fred Aldous
37 Lever Street
Manchester M1 1LW
www.fredaldous.co.uk
Tel: 01612 364224
*Wide range of craft
equipment, including a good
selection of decorative-
edged scissors*

Hobbycraft
www.hobbycraft.co.uk
*Wide range of craft
equipment and papers*

Lawrence Art Supplies
Shops in Hove and Redruth,
Cornwall
Tel: 0845 644 3232
www.lawrence.co.uk
*Artists' materials and a good
range of papers, including
many handmade
Japanese varieties*

Paperchase
213–215 Tottenham
Court Road
London W1T 7PS
Tel: 020 7467 6200
www.paperchase.co.uk
*Extensive range of decorative
and plain papers*

The Paper Warehouse
Grosvenor House Papers Ltd
Westmorland Business Park
Kendal LA9 6NP
Tel: 01539 726161
Email: info@ghpkendal.co.uk
www.ghpkendal.co.uk
*General craft retailer of a
wide range of papercraft
supplies, including punches
and peel-offs*

Squires Model and Craft Tools
100 London Road
Bognor Regis
West Sussex PO21 1DD
Tel: 01243 842424
*Exhaustive range of art and
craft papers, also model
makers' tools including
traditional and rotating knives
and traditional/decorative-
edged scissors*

Streets Ahead Dollshouse
Unit 6 Bell Park
Bell Close
Newham Industrial Estate
Plympton
Plymouth
Devon PL7 4JH
Tel: 01752 338222
Email: sales@sa-imports.co.uk
*Supplier of printed doll's
house papers; contact for
details of stockists*

US Suppliers

Fascinating Folds
PO Box 10070
Glendale AZ 85318
www.fascinating-folds.com
*An extensive supplier of
reference materials
for papercraft*

Hollander's Decorative and Handmade Papers
410 N Fourth Avenue
Ann Arbor MI 48104
Tel: 734 741 7531
www.hollanders.com
*Supplier of unique decorative
papers plus stationery*

Paperarts
www.paperarts.com (Arizona)
*Wide range of
exciting papers*

Paper Mojo
www.papermojo.com
Tel: 1 800 420 3818

Twinrocker Handmade Paper
100 East 3rd Street
Brookston IN 47923
Tel: 765 563 3119
www.twinrocker.com
*Supplier of handmade
paper and importer of
decorative papers*

Acknowledgments

I would like to thank everyone who helped me to produce this book, especially Cheryl Brown for her enthusiasm and for thinking it was a good idea in the first place; Karl Adamson for his great step photography, and for driving so far; Siiri Skerker for her fine hospitality; Sarah Underhill for her lovely styling and art direction; Kim Sayer for his great finished shots; Mia Farrant for layout; Jo Richardson for effortlessly sorting it all out; and Beth Dymond for pulling it all together at the end. Many thanks also to Iain and Wendy for allowing me to use their photograph. Most thanks, and love, go to Neil and Stella, as ever, for putting up with it all.

About the Author

Marion Elliot works in a variety of materials, especially paper and fabric. She is an avid collector of vintage fabrics, buttons and knitting patterns, and haunts her local charity shops. She is very keen on recycling and reworking her finds into new and beautiful items, and you can catch up with her at her Etsy shop to see what she's been up to:
www.etsy.com.
http://vintagetown.etsy.com

Index